A Saturday Night Soldier's War
1913–1918

NORMAN TENNANT

*Designed by Peter Tucker, typeset in Bembo
and printed at the Alden Press, Oxford
All rights reserved*

*The Kylin Press, Darbonne House, Waddesdon, Buckinghamshire
© The Kylin Press, 1983
ISBN 0 907128 11 4*

Dedication

Dedicated to all my *'Saturday Night Soldier'* friends of the 11th Howitzer Battery, (later known as D/245 Battery) 49th West Riding Territorial Division and particularly to those signallers who shared with me throughout three years of the First World War, the bitter frustration of laying and maintaining, in impossible conditions, the miles of telephone cables on the Western Front.

Especially would I honour the treasured memory of those who did not come home, together with those many survivors who have since answered the *'Last Call'* and left me a lonely *'Old Sweat'*.

Having known them so well I feel that my friends, though sometimes the victims of my light-hearted caricatures, would have shown no resentment.

N.T.
September 1983

This is copy no

403.

of a special edition
of five hundred copies
signed by the author

Norman Tennant

Contents

Introduction 1
1913: *The King's Shilling* 3
1914: *Embodiment* 7
1915: *Into action* 13
1916: *Preparing for the Somme Offensive* 36
1917: *Useless slaughter on the Somme* 70
1918: *Things look rather black* 114

Introduction

In the normal course of events, the number of people who can remember the conditions of life in those far-off days before the First World War, grows smaller each year. For them the task of describing to others those conditions in mere words, is naturally almost impossible, since words can only convey meanings which lie within the experience of each individual.

To me the atmosphere of those pre-1914 days can be brought to mind by the memory of the gentle splashing of a public fountain opposite my parents house and the quiet murmur of the beck which supplied it, before running under the street down to the river. It was a refreshing sound during the long hot days of summer in a quietness and secure peace now, alas, unknown and the occasional clip-clop of horse carriages did nothing to disturb the calm.

Winter with six or eight inches of snow on the ground could be even quieter, since road traffic was either muted or stopped altogether and the only sounds were the scrape of shovels as men tried to clear the roads and footpaths.

It was such indications as these of the leisurely tempo of life which heralded the world-wide unrest of the early years of the century and brought the reality of war into clearer perspective bringing with it a growing sense of purpose to all local Territorial Army units.

Stationed throughout the United Kingdom these units differed from the Regular Army in that they consisted of officers and men who knew each other intimately in civilian life. Their discipline was derived more from a sense of comradeship than from the methods normally employed by the Regular Army. There was a friendly rivalry with other neighbouring Territorial units which inspired a team spirit that was to be so valuable in the coming years.

It was not until 1916 that I was prevailed upon to keep a diary and after several weeks of stumbling amateur effort, I was able to fill the pages with closely written, factual, day-to-day record of events upon which this account is mainly based.

Before that I have relied on memory and many of my own photographs and press cuttings to render an unvarnished account of the life of one soldier in the Territorial Army of 1913, 1914 and 1915.

Looking back over the war years, I can hardly believe that the Battery which took an active part in practically every major battle on the western front, should have escaped with such a relatively small casualty list of 96.

From Aubers Ridge in May 1915 followed by six months to the end of that year in the Ypres Salient, the Somme, Beaumont Hamel, Arras, Vimy Ridge, Nieuport and Passchendaele all figured in the Battery's battle honours.

The original strength of the Battery was 143 officers, NCOs and men, to be augmented to approximately 215 in 1917 when the unit was increased from 4 to 6 guns. Although 96 casualties appear to be almost half of the total strength the list is very small compared with the massive scale of slaughter in 1914–1918 and seemed to imply that we enjoyed what was termed a *cushy* time. But reference to the Battery history Record of D/245 Battery 1914–1919 by Sergeant A.E. Gee MM and Corporal A.E. Shaw, published by Renwick of Otley and now, I hope, to the following pages, quickly disproves that.

This remarkable good fortune was in no small part due to the care and devotion to his men by the Battery Commander, Major P.C. Petrie DSO, MC who had helped to raise it, train it and command it to the end of the war.

So here is the plain unvarnished record of one of *The Saturday Night Soldiers* who had the good fortune to serve as a signaller in D/245 Battery.

1913: *The King's Shilling*

Together with some of my school friends who had just left the Grammar School at Ilkley I enlisted, under the legal age, in the local Territorial Army unit which was the 11th Battery, 4th West Riding Howitzer brigade, Royal Field Artillery and became one of that national joke *The Saturday Night Soldiers*.

To the great dismay of my parents I arrived home one evening with a kit-bag full of uniforms and equipment, in pocket to the sum of one shilling — *The King's Shilling*.

On Saturday nights we were trained at the local drill hall in the use of the rifle and the 5 inch howitzer together with the painful acquisition of a precarious seat in the saddle on a wide variety of horses hired from the local tradesmen.

Weekend training camps were held in the district at Whitsuntide and a further fortnight under canvas in August at some more distant spot afforded an opportunity for the whole Brigade, of which the units were stationed in several different towns, to train together.

It was at my first weekend camp that I was given a timely reminder that our heavy vehicles were to be treated with the utmost respect and I was saved from a messy end by the presence of mind of our skilled, veteran Sergeant-instructor *Josey Loveridge* who was supervising a tricky S turn from the narrow road into a field where the camp was situated.

The entrance was a gate set in a slight hollow and it was no easy task to manoeuvre a six horse team with its gun and limber through it. The gunners who

Much to my parents dismay I enlisted in the Royal Field Artillery

Almost crushed to a jelly before the outbreak of War

dismounted from the limber and waited on the road until their vehicle was safely through.

Just as my gun was in a right hand turn I noticed some equipment falling off the limber and started forward to retrieve it. I was brought up short with the agonising feeling that all my guts were being forced through my backbone as the sergeant who had been standing behind me grabbed the belt of my greatcoat and pulled me back. He gave me a severe lecture on the dangers of going between the limber and the gun as the wide space on the right hand turn would be reduced to nothing on the left hand turn which followed and I would have been crushed to a jelly.

In August the whole Brigade was encamped in a vast field near Bow Street station a few miles from Aberystwyth.

Long lines of bell tents accommodated the men and marquees were erected for QM stores, officers, sergeants and men's messes. It was a new experience for us to be working and eating with the men of the other Battery of the Brigade and the Ammunition Column and to this day the smell of crushed grass, which is always to be found inside marquees, reminds me of those rough and ready meals on the bare trestle tables, slightly flavoured with smoke from the cookhouse fires nearby.

During the second week we trekked up into the hills near Plynlimon for a firing course and, as it was mostly uphill, the gunners had to march behind the guns and wagons instead of riding on the limbers. It was a hot summer and clouds of choking dust were thrown up from the

rough country roads by the grinding iron rimmed wheels and the hooves of the six horse gun and wagon teams. Parched and weary it was a welcome relief to pull off the road onto level grassy moorland where we bivouacced for the night.

Next day the guns were brought into action ready to fire our first live shells, the target being an old bell tent on the hillside about a mile away. Dragshoes were set behind each gun wheel and attached by chains to the hub because, on firing, the small recoil buffers were unable to prevent the whole gun from leaping back several feet.

The layer would mount his sight in the socket provided, set the range and angle of deflection from an aiming post set some yards in front, then elevate the gun barrel as required and get the whole contraption pointing in the right direction by signalling with his hand to the *'number one'* who would lift and move the heavy trail by means of a handspike set in a socket.

Meanwhile the fuse on the first shell was being set to burst either in the air after so many seconds or on percussion when the fuse was turned to mark P.

The loader was about to push the shell into the breech when the Regular Army Adjutant shouted 'Stop' and came up to check the fuse setting. Now the fuse had been set in the error at 0 seconds instead of at P for percussion which meant that on firing the shell would have burst in the gun or just as it left the muzzle and there would have been a most regrettable and messy accident. Needless to say that particular mistake was never repeated.

It was fascinating to observe for the first time the devastating effect of our 5 inch shells bursting in the target area but rather disappointing to see the bell tent still standing at the end of the day. Perhaps this was hardly surprising since our weapons were the old Boer War B.L. Howitzers; the letters BL stood for Breech Loading and seemed to imply that it was a desirable improvement on a muzzle loader. One of these pieces of ordnance belonging to our sister battery, the 10th, is now in the Imperial War Museum – a fitting place for it.

It was natural that groups of school friends should be drawn together, in addition to making new contacts, and this continued throughout the war. In due course we came to appreciate the sterling qualities of some of the rougher local types and to respond to their innate friendliness but here in our first annual camp we felt rather shy in their presence and tended to associate with those we already knew so well.

While exploring the area with several of my friends after the day's exercises were over, we found a small farm where they provided us with a splendid meal of tea, home made bread, scones and cakes, cream and jam – it was gooseberry jam I remember. When we asked them how much we owed they were reluctant to take anything, but finally and with hesitation wondered if sixpence each would be too much.

In addition to the khaki outfit of tunic, riding breeches with leather patches on the inside of the leg and puttees rolled downwards and tied with the tape at the ankle instead of the infantry method of starting at the ankles and finishing with the tape below the knee, we had a splendid dress uniform. This consisted of a dark blue tunic with gold braid trimmings and stiff upright collar, trousers with a broad red stripe strapped under the instep and braced up so tight that bending became a difficult and dangerous operation, walking out boots fitted with swan necked spurs and a cap with a stiff shiny black peak.

Parades and gun-drill were not too strenuous and on free afternoons we would catch a train to Aberstwyth to display our gorgeous uniforms and enjoy more civilised food in the cafes.

Major Petrie (left) and Lieutenant Eddison with our Boer War five inch Breech Loading Howitzer

1914: *Embodiment*

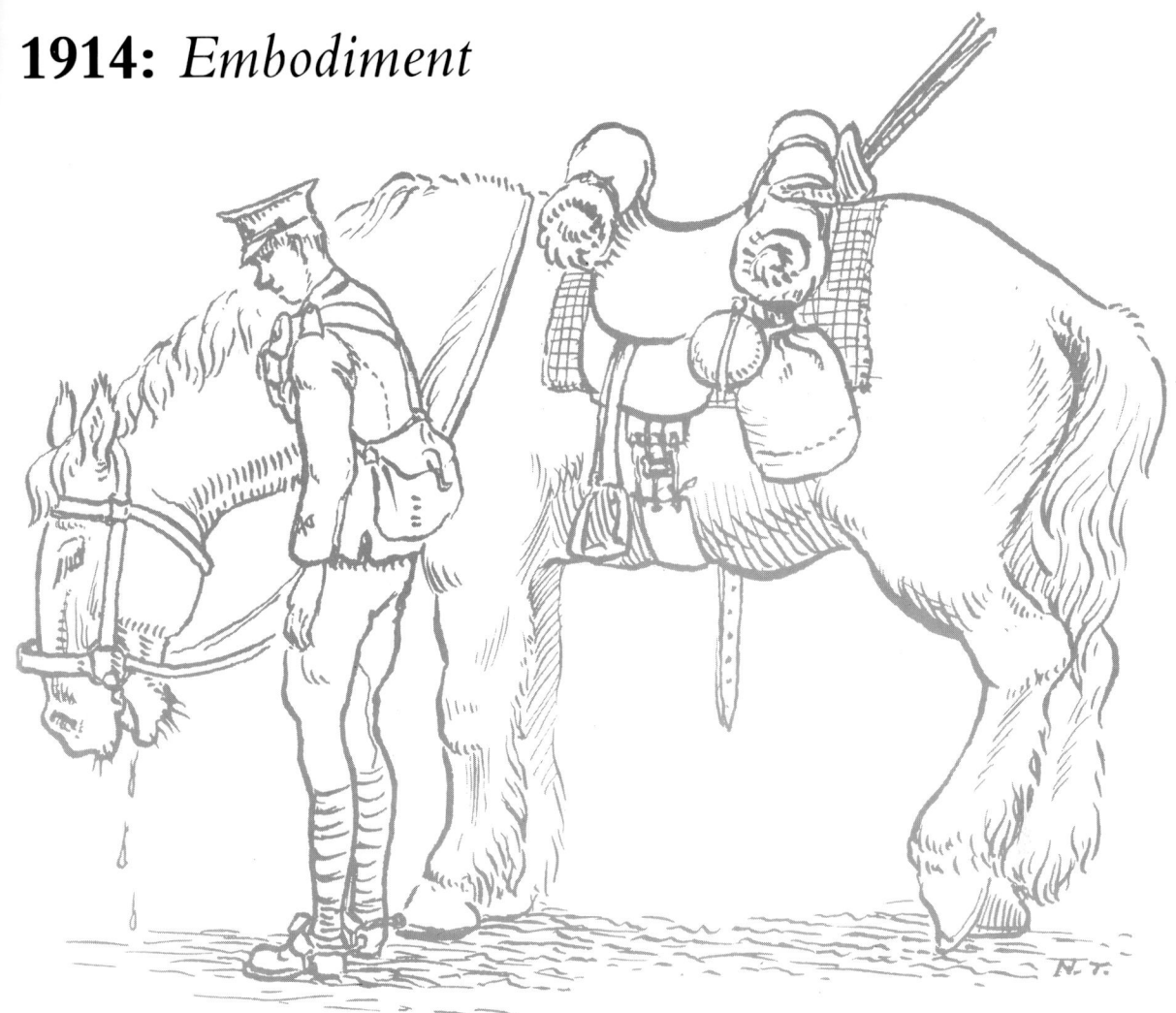

My 'spare wheeler'— his girth bridged with string

IN THE AUGUST of 1914 the annual camp was held at Pembrey, South Wales and, together with some of my friends, I volunteered to go with the advance party to prepare the camp.

We were issued with coarse canvas jackets and trousers and were initiated into the correct methods of erecting bell tents and marquees, digging latrines and unloading trestle tables and forms. It was all very pleasant and informal and we thoroughly enjoyed it. No sooner had the main body arrived a few days later than war was declared and the Brigade had to return home.

This seemed to be the real thing and when my Embodiment Notice arrived by post the following day I felt that now we were irrevocably committed to the unknown. Reporting at the drill hall we were kitted up in preparation for a move to Brigade HQ at the neighbouring town of Otley where we were billetted in a school. Having no horses the guns and wagons were hauled by two of the council's steam rollers, each one pulling two guns and four wagons with their limbers all lashed together — surely we must have been the first mechanised unit!

Here we collected enough horses for all the vehicles and for the outriders — i.e. NCOs, rangefinders, signallers, — yes, and trumpeters. Then we moved as a complete Brigade to Doncaster to join the rest of the 49th West Riding Division.

Here we slept in the long double row of stables behind the racecourse grandstand while the horses were picketed out in the centre of the course. Later when the weather became colder the horses were brought in under cover in the stables and the men were moved up into the grandstand building.

Training as a division was carried out in the surrounding country where manoeuvres brought an exhilarating sense of freedom when riding over the fields in defiance of the normal laws of trespass.

As the Territorial Force was originally formed for home defence every man was afforded the opportunity to volunteer for service overseas or to remain in this country. Practically all volunteered and a small metal badge with the words *Imperial Service*, probably unofficial, made its appearance and was worn by many. It seemed quite illogical but, I suppose, in keeping with the signs *Business as usual* which appeared on most shops and businesses when the Brigade was moved under canvas to Sandbeck Park to enable the St. Leger to be held at Doncaster racecourse.

It was here that we were joined by a number of recruits in their civilian clothes and a real *ragtime* lot we looked.

Back in Doncaster our training went steadily on as the fine days of autumn gave way to winter conditions. Guard duty over the vehicles of the whole Brigade parked in the big square behind the grandstand came round at intervals; the guardroom was a tiny one storey building in the corner of the square which served as a police station complete with cells during race meetings. Mounting the guard became a much more ceremonial affair and during the hours of daylight one had to be particularly alert or the fiery little Regimental Sergeant-major would spot any slackness from the window of his office overlooking the square and come striding out in a towering rage.

At first the nights seemed eerie and full of strange sounds and stealthy footsteps; a sudden bumping disturbance accompanied by screams turned out to be kicking horses in some nearby stable. A visit by the Orderly Officer when the guard had to be called out and inspected helped to pass a little time.

Another guard had occasionally to be provided at a small store behind the High Street in the town. The sentry stood at the entry of a narrow passage leading to the store and his daylight hours were made miserable by having to salute all passing officers; it was always an anxious time trying to spot the badges of rank and to determine if the officer could be saluted by slapping the rifle butt with the right hand while at the slope or whether he held a rank which demanded a 'Present arms'.

This last little ceremony always had to be carried out for any passing armed body of troops and it was no small ordeal to stand at the *'present'* while section after section of a battery of artillery would return the compliment by bellowing out *'Eyes right'* or *'Eyes left'* according to which way they were going.

One felt very important when every officer in turn saluted, every driver brought his whip vertically in front of his face and then cut it away to hold it over the withers of his offside horse; every gunner sat up straight with arms folded and all turned the head to look at one in passing until the final *'Eyes front'* order brought relief from this concentrated stare which was sometimes an obvious jeer.

Training of the parade ground type was sometimes given beyond the Great North Road, now the A1 on a large open space since developed as a football ground.

On one of these occasions the Battery was advancing with its four guns in line abreast followed by the battery wagons, first line wagons and battery staff of which, as a signaller, I was a member; three lines of vehicles each drawn by its team of six horses made quite a formidable array. Then came the order *'Battery will retire'* at which each vehicle wheeled about in its own length and moved in the opposite direction. This sharp turn unsettled my inexpert seat in the saddle and I lost my stirrups and my balance. All I had left to hold on by were my spurs and my long-suffering mount, taking the prick of my spurs as the usual signal for more speed, leapt forward to my further discomfort and quickly overtook each line of vehicles in turn. Now the only figure in front of me was the OC riding alone, up to that moment, in all his majesty. As I was carried past him I was dimly aware of a puzzled look directed at me but with tactful restraint he said nothing — not even *'goodbye'*. It was a great relief to me and no less to my horse when a little further on I fell off.

At the near end of the row of stables behind the grandstand was a small cottage occupied, presumably, by one of the racecourse employees; this man and his wife started making coffee in the early mornings and later kept a stock of cakes and biscuits.

It was a big help to us in getting up for early morning stables to know that a piping hot drink was ready, indeed it was always so hot that it couldn't be consumed straight away. The cold winter darkness must have hidden many a steaming cup while the sergeant of each subsection called the roll by the light of a hurricane lamp.

On December 16th a German naval force crept in under cover of mist and darkness and fired a few shells on Scarborough. It was suspected that an invasion might be imminent and the Brigade *'Stood to'* all night with the teams hooked into the vehicles ready to move off.

Life was still present

My usual mount was commandeered to replace a sick horse in the gun team and I was given a '*spare wheeler*'. Now a team consisted of six horses, two light draught in the lead, two medium draught in the centre and two heavy draught in the rear — '*wheelers*' they were called and '*spare wheelers*' were usually the dregs of the equine establishment. The dreg I got was a vast immobile brute with thick hairy legs and drooping head; it seemed quite happy to spend most of its existence standing perfectly still, an occasional tremor of its lower bearded lip indicated that life was still present. To take this creature to water with one other normally eager horse was to suffer all the agonies of the rack.

My saddle with all its attached equipment, i.e. rolled greatcoat in front, rolled blanket behind, nosebag containing food (for the horse), hay net, mess tin, rifle bucket containing signalling flags (which always prevented the right leg from being thrown smartly over the saddle in mounting) and sundry odds and ends was somehow hoisted onto the beast's back; I'm not sure that we didn't use a ladder. Of course the girth wouldn't meet underneath so the gap was bridged with string and I passed the night alongside praying that our help in saving Scarborough wouldn't be needed. It wasn't!

Our '*walking out dress*', as our second khaki uniform was called, received a certain amount of unofficial attention. The leather pieces on the inside of our riding breeches were replaced by buckskin and kept pipeclayed and the outside seams were cut into a more dashing Mountie shape; tunics were more smartly tailored and the swan necked spurs fitted with tin discs in the rowels to give a jingle when the heel met the ground in walking.

Chromium chains under the instep gave a sparkle and clasp knife round the left shoulder were pipeclayed. All this nonsense was very soon to end.

The first Christmas I had ever spent

away from the family with its homely festivities and exchange of gifts came and passed without my having the slightest recollection of events. It might be supposed that I was too drunk to remember but it so happened that I detested the taste of beer and any alcoholic drink and was one of the few who remained teetotal throughout the whole war, even to the extent of refusing the rum ration.

In February 1915 the Brigade entrained for a firing course on Salisbury Plain, arriving at Amesbury station in the middle of a cold and rainy night. Rollestone Camp was a vast sea of mud and wooden hutments and it was here that I engendered a lasting hate for the inimical menace of army camps.

Out on the range next day we prepared to fire our allotted ration of live rounds. The OC took his party forward and to a flank to observe and correct the fire, the corrections being signalled back to the Battery by semaphore. Our position was on the crest of hill from which we had a good view of the target on the opposite hillside; below us were some small buildings.

Number one gun fired and we watched a fountain of earth rise near the target. Corrections were signalled back and number two gun ordered to fire. With our eyes on the target waiting for the burst we became aware of something rushing towards us at great speed and before we realised what it was the thing, a 56 lb shell, had exploded with a roar just beyond the building below us. Some unfortunate gunlayer had got the wrong deflection on his sight.

Towards the end of our stay in Doncaster we had a temporary OC posted to the Battery who was responsible for depriving me of my embarkation leave as the following episode explains.

Each of the booths behind the grandstand buildings held 4 or 5 horses and the one in which I worked included a vicious kicker which had caused a nasty injury on the leg of the horse next to it. One day at '*Mid-day Stables*', a parade which was always attended by the OC and which dragged on interminably as we groomed and curry combed and tended our mounts, this kicker became temperamental again and lashed out at its neighbour's leg.

Seizing a broom I had just raised it to deliver an admonitory clout on its rump when the OC's party on its long round of inspection suddenly appeared at the open door. In attendance with the Major was

'Sergeant-Major, take that man's name'

the section commander, the sergeant-major, the farrier-sergeant and the sergeant in charge of our sub-section.

A moment's horrified silence then the OC purple with rage, screamed 'Sergeant-major take that man's name'. I think what hurt me most was having to state my name to the BSM – that well loved Billy Brown who was perfectly familiar with the name of every man in the Battery; I felt that I had disappointed this kindly man in some way.

At the Orderly Room I was awarded 14 days CB, thus forfeiting my embarkation leave of four days which was almost due. I scrubbed floors and stone steps; peeled potatoes by the hundredweight and all the rest of the dire punishment. If I had not written home to ask my parents to send a telegram requesting my presence on 'Urgent family affairs', I would not have had any leave at all before going abroad; as it was I managed to wangle 48 hours at home to say my goodbyes.

1915: *Into action*

We left for France on the 14th April. The rail journey to the port of embarkation took place at night and was shrouded in mystery; there was an air of excitement, a sense of great events pending and a certain relief mixed with regret that the long days of training at Doncaster were over.

Shipping the guns, wagons, horses and stores took most of the following day and was marred by an unfortunate accident. One of the guns of our sister battery, the 10th, slipped out of its slings, crashing down onto the dock and injuring two men.

Approaching the harbour at Le Havre next morning we were fascinated by the French scene with its strange houses, vehicles, people and smells. After unloading we were given a meal in one of the dock sheds and later we harnessed up the teams and pulled out through the dark cobbled streets to the station where the vehicles were run onto flat trucks and the horses and men packed into vans. There seemed to be endless waiting but at last as day was breaking we started our train journey to the unknown.

The leisurely progress through the French countryside was enjoyable as everything was so new to us — even the telegraph poles were a different shape and made of concrete instead of wood. How badly kept and full of weeds the permanent way seemed compared with the trim railways at home and the station platforms looked ridiculously low and near the track.

We detrained at a small station called

'We began to sense a sort of warning that our romantic conception of war might be displaced'

Berguette and took the road to St. Venant which wound its way through the fields and orchards gay with spring blossom. Passing through hamlets and past farms and cottages we were greeted by smiling women and children and a few old men.

Near St. Venant we were billetted in several farms, the vehicles parked in a meadow and the horses tethered to a line stretched between wagon wheels. After watering at a nearby pond there followed the interminable grooming ending with the long awaited order *'Stand to your feeds'*. The horses soon got to know this order and would whinny and move about excitedly and look back over their shoulders to the men standing in a line, each with two filled nosebags.

At the order *'Feed'* each man would be

faced with the problem of how to feed two hungry horses at once. The nosebag had to be lifted over the horse's mouth, the strap pushed over the ears and tightened if necessary. But when the animal is moving about, and thrusting its nose down to the ground to bring the contents of the bag within reach of its mouth, it is no easy matter, particularly as the other horse waiting its turn impatiently is trying to get its head into the second nosebag hanging over one's shoulder.

When at last they were all eating happily the sub-sections fell in behind, the numbers one reported '*All fed*' and then came the long awaited '*Dismiss*' followed by a wild rush to collect mess tins and line up at the temporary cookhouse for a meal.

The low rumble of distant gunfire could occasionally be heard and the war for which we had been training for so long became more of a reality. We hadn't had enough experience yet for fear to enter into our consciousness, but we began to sense a sort of warning that our romantic conceptions of war might be misplaced. It did not prevent us however from welcoming the move up to the line — a move which, later in the war, we came to loathe and dread.

Our operations as a division never seemed to bring us into very close contact with the other arms such as the infantry, engineers, R.A.S.C. or even the other field batteries. We would see them about, of course, but their connection with us seemed to be remote and the life of our unit was completely insulated; nothing was real beyond our immediate locality and companions but I suspect that this incurious acceptance of a world limited to our narrow surroundings may have been purely personal. For instance I was not aware at the time that for our first operation the two howitzer batteries were detached from the divison and sent to add what in those early days amounted to considerable fire power to the Aubers Ridge offensive which was intended to break through to Lille.

We moved up to Richebourg St. Vaast

'Feed'

and pushed the guns into position behind a hedge while we were billetted in the village school until we could erect shelters on the position.

Then followed our first experience of building dug-outs which really were built rather than excavated owing to the marshy nature of the flat country in those parts. We filled sandbags until we ached in every joint and we just hated to see each one hammered flat with the back of a spade as it was laid in position, it seemed to require so many more sandbags to make a wall that way.

Corrugated iron sheets were not available in those days and we had to roof over our shelters with doors and any timber we could scrounge from the shattered buildings in the village. These were covered with sandbags and earth and were only splinter or shrapnel proof. Sandbag blast walls were erected round each gun and camouflaged with branches which quickly died and would have provided no concealment from later aerial photography.

The war lords were still trying to wage trench warfare with shrapnel instead of high explosive and one indication of their slow absorption of ideas, or maybe it was a lack of suitable ordnance, was the presence in a nearby orchard of an Indian mountain battery firing away its ridiculous little squibs.

While we occupied that position no enemy shells fell very near except on one occasion when a machine gun team arrived and opened indirect fire on some distant target. Whether by exceptional skill or pure chance I don't know but the first few rounds from our guns brought immediate retaliation in the form of a shell which scored a direct hit from our guns killing the sergeant and effectively discouraging the plan. As several more shells fell amongst our guns we were relieved when the machine gunners left.

The first trip forward to our observation post was made by the O.C. accompanied by another signaller and myself to find a suitable route for a telephone line between the O.P. and the Battery. Following a road which cut across the front of our position for 500 yards we turned right towards the trenches.

About a quarter of a mile down was a road block by a farm occupied by a battalion H.Q. Standing at this block was one of the few German prisoners I ever saw at close quarters — a fine chap with a big blonde beard and it was strange to think that this inoffensive looking man was one of the *fire-eating toughs* we were supposed to be fighting.

Leaving the road at this point we moved behind the farm buildings into an orchard. It was here that we heard for the first time the scream of a hostile shell. We dived behind a big pear tree and then got up rather quickly feeling very ashamed as the shell fell quite a long way off. With more experience we were able to gauge the approximate dropping point of any high angle shells which were more leisurely in the early stages of their flight. We realised after a time that we would not hear the ones with our names on nor would we get any warning of high velocity shells coming towards us. It happened on several later occasions that we saw a H.V. shell burst followed by the sound of its explosion, the shriek of its approach and then the faint pop of the distant gun which had fired it, in that order.

From the moment of hearing the first shell throughout the next three years we always moved about with our ears at the alert; it became a subconscious state of readiness to take evasive action which underlay all our conscious thoughts and movements.

After passing through the orchard we followed hedges and tracks to a ruined factory in the village of Richebourg l'Avoué which lay just behind the front line. Beyond the factory was a wide open space traversed by a low breastwork providing cover till we reached the village street, where from one of the cottage upper rooms, we could get a view over the flat countryside.

The ground in front was cut up by bits of breastwork and barbed wire entanglements and appeared to be quite deserted. Occasionally a shell would throw up a fountain of dirt and debris and single rifle shots or short bursts of machine gun fire would break the brooding stillness.

After dark that night a working party went down to construct a dug-out behind the cottage while the signallers laid a telephone line from the Battery to the O.P. The wire was laid loose along the side of ditches and hedges but had to be carried over roads and tracks on poles or trees when available.

It was most uncanny at first working in the dark with a succession of verey lights rising and falling over the branches making the shadows of ruined walls and broken trees move over the ground. Occasional sounds of ration parties stumbling and clinking their way up to the front line, or stretcher bearers coming back, would break the stillness and all this furtive movement and secret activity became a regular feature during the hours of darkness.

The next day the guns were registered on their targets and one by one the range and deflection corrections conveyed by field telephone so that the Battery could fire on any target at any time when required by the infantry in our particular sector. Artillery support was always there in response to pre-arranged rocket signals. Our battery-powered telephones could either send morse signals by means of a buzzer or by speech through a folding receiver and microphone.

We thought it might be a good idea to try visual signalling from the O.P. in case the telephone line failed and one night we carried out a test of messages in morse by means of a torch directed through a length of drainpipe which had been aligned onto a pre-arranged spot in daylight. On the opposite side of the road from the O.P. cottage was another house and it was from the roof of an outhouse behind this that we started our signals. The glare of light from the end of our drainpipe was rather alarming in the dark but we got one answering flash and then no more. Later we heard that the signallers at the Battery end had been arrested as spies but were soon released after explanations were accepted.

In this sector there were a number of Indian troops and it was interesting to watch the different races such as the Sikhs, tall, bearded, dignified and aloof winding yards and yards of turban into a neat headdress; the little Gurkhas with their quick movements and flashing smiles carrying their special weapon the *kukri* with which they were said to be adept at despatching German sentries.

The various duties involved quickly made it apparent that the number of signallers on the strength was quite inadequate and the director and rangefinder men together with the two trumpeters were brought in to help.

Having laid field lines to Brigade H.Q. the O.P. and the officers mess — a minimum which was often more than doubled later on — they then had to be maintained against shell fire, traffic and the constant passage of men down the trenches where lines were laid. The telephones at the Battery end had to be manned day and night and we usually worked in pairs taking the different duties in rotation. At the O.P. two were necessary in case of a breakdown so that one could reply to a test made by the other at any break he might find in the line. Both broken ends had to be tested before joining them up and binding with insulation tape to make sure there was no other fault.

The attack was due to open at dawn on May 9th and the O.P. was manned before this so that fire from the Battery could be controlled when the infantry had captured the trench system in front as they confidently expected to do. In the event the attack was held up by the wire entanglements which were supposed to have been cut by shrapnel and we suffered heavy losses.

This first experience of action was

Field lines had to be maintained against shellfire, traffic and the constant passage of men

A vivid flash and a tremendous blow on the nose

exciting in its novelty and the sound of so many of our shells falling onto the German trenches a little way in front of our cottage must have lulled me into a false feeling of security, making the approach of hostile shells sound very similar to our own as I found to my cost.

It was my companion's turn on the telephone and I was standing in the open doorway watching supporting infantry file past down the street to where they entered a communication trench at the end of our row of cottages. Suddenly there was a vivid flash and I felt what appeared to be a tremendous blow on the nose which knocked me back into the cottage and then, somehow, I found that I was lying against the wall.

Putting my hand up to see if my tingling head was still there I saw to my horror that my fingers were covered with blood. My head felt numb and I thought that I must be dead. However someone put on a field dressing and I was able to walk back to the Battery.

I was extremely lucky because the same shell killed one of the passing infantry and wounded another. It certainly cured me of idle curiosity and taught me a lot about the potentialities of high explosive. The wound was a trifling one and after an anti-tetanus injection, a fresh dressing and a night's rest, I was on duty again. It was completely thoughtless on my part not to have mentioned this incident when I wrote home because some idiot had to include it in a letter which was published in the local paper causing great distress and anxiety to my parents when they read about it until I could reassure them that the wound was quite a trivial one.

Another unsuccessful attempt to capture Aubers Ridge was made a week later and soon after that we left Richebourg.

Richebourg O.P. May 9th 1915

Pulling out of a position was always attended by mixed feelings of relief at going away from trouble and acute anxiety at the possibility of being shelled while the gun teams were milling about the position. On a still night it sounded as if the shouted orders and jingling harness could be heard in Berlin.

Each gun would be man-handled out of its emplacement, then the six horse team would have to drive over the end of the trail, swing round at right angles and halt as soon as the limber wheel had passed over the trail so that the gunners could lift it up onto the hook on the limber. This entailed some careful judgement on the part of the drivers as the operation invariably took place in darkness.

We moved away to rejoin our division which was in a quiet sector of the line near Fleurbaix. For some reason this part of the front remained comparatively peaceful up to the German offensive in 1918 and divisions which had received a gruelling time in the more murderous areas were sent here to recuperate.

Our new position at La Croix Marechal was in an orchard bordering one of the many minor roads which formed quite a network in this district. On the roadside stood several cottages still occupied and it was characteristic of this region that French civilians were allowed to come round with little hand-carts selling fruit and chocolate. One could buy coffee at any cottage as the coffee pot was always simmering on the flat flue of the stove which often stood out in the centre of the room. In one place we were given eggs which had been boiled in the coffee so we didn't go there any more.

There was an almost peaceful atmosphere in this place and the occasional

'Snipers' — an incident at Fleurboir

shell came almost as an insult. One day a party of men were busy with picks and spades burying a telephone line across the entrance to a field when suddenly a rifle shot broke the stillness. It sounded very close but we carried on, nobody liking to be the first to drop flat, until another whipcrack indicated that, as we suspected, we were the target of deliberate shooting and as one man we dived for cover. The shots came from somewhere much nearer than the trenches and we came to the conclusion that it must have been a sniper concealed behind our line; several of these had already been rounded up.

Our O.P. was in a large villa or convent standing in an overgrown ornamental garden on the fringe of Bois Grenier, a village lying about a kilometre north of the Battery. To reach it we made use of the messcart, a one-horse vehicle like a Victorian milk float, which brought the rations and mail up from the wagon line each day. This in itself was a clear indication of the comparatively untroubled state of the war here.

Bois Grenier was near the front line

and all the civilians had been evacuated; there was a most uncanny stillness about everything and one felt uneasy and threatened.

This leisurely war was bound to come to an end soon and one night we pulled out of our position under the apple trees at La Croix Marechal. After a night at the wagon line where we renewed acquaintance with the drivers and others we moved to an unknown destination.

These moves were always a matter of conjecture although someone was sure to know exactly where we were bound. Nobody worried or cared much about it until later in the war when we would hope that we might be taken out for a rest and prayed that we were not heading for another of the dreaded hot spots of the front. On this occasion we moved across the frontier into Belgium and stopped at Watou next to a field of hops growing on poles, something which was quite strange to most of us north countrymen.

Our journey up to the gun position took us through Poperinghe and Vlamertinghe, turning north before reaching Ypres to Brielen.

Just beyond this village was an estaminet called Herberg de Kroone which was still occupied by a Belgian family consisting of old *Hookna-harkna* as we

'A one-horse vehicle like a Victorian milk float'

The wagon line became churned into a sea of mud

called him after the sound of his incomprehensible Flemish, his wife and two sons who went out to work somewhere every day.

Most of the Battery personnel were billetted in the loft while the officers took over a small cottage nearby. The gunners and signallers on duty lived in dugouts on the gun position which was sited on the far edge of a large cornfield.

The Herberg de Kroone remained intact during our six months occupation but soon after we left we learnt that a heavy shell had wrecked the roadside part of the upper storey where the sergeants' mess had been. Between the road and the house ran the single track, now overgrown on which used to run the steam trams with their trailing coaches which usually followed the main roads but sometimes struck across country.

It was always interesting to discover what daylight revealed of our surroundings after a night move into a new position.

Standing on the tree-lined road which ran from Ypres through Brielen to Elverdinghe and the north, we could see the Battery straight ahead beyond the cornfield dug in behind a hedge dotted with pollard willows. On the left flank near D sub-section gun, as a constant reminder

of the war, was a huge shell hole probably made by one of the 'Jack Johnsons' which reduced Ypres to such desolation. In front of the Battery a piece of waste ground led to a narrow strip of woodland which served to screen the gun flashes from enemy observation.

Looking left from the Herberg the road passed a large farm occupied by one of the field gun batteries of the division; 15 pounders they were at that time until they were replaced by 18 pounders in January 1916 when we were re-armed with the new 4.5 inch howitzer. One of the guns of this battery was placed in a barn and was known as 'the barn door cock' because the concealing barn doors had to be thrown open when firing took place.

A little way past this farm a road turned right leading down to Boesinghe and the trenches; a hundred yards beyond was a road used by teams coming up from the wagon line. Not far beyond lay the village of Elverdinghe where parties used to be sent at night to collect loads of bricks and rubble from the shattered buildings to be used as horse standings as the wagon line became churned into a sea of mud.

To the right of the Herberg were two cottages and then lying back from the road, an occupied farm. '*Mucky Farm*' we called it and *mucky* it was. The farm kitchen swarmed with flies and the butter which could be bought for 5 francs per kilo contained a large proportion of dead ones but we seemed to find it worth risking. Running alongside the farm was an avenue leading to the Chateau des Trois Tours used as some sort of H.Q. and for some mysterious reason it was never shelled. Just past the entrance to the avenue was a mound on which stood the ruins of a windmill and then the first houses in the village street.

The Herberg de Kroone was built at right angles to the road; first came the public room with its corner door, never used now, then the bedrooms of the family and the kitchen and then a sort of earth floored workshop from which a flight of steps led up to the attics where the men slept. Beyond this towards the front of the building were several smaller rooms partitioned off and papered with newspapers and used by the sergeants and the medical orderly and the Battery Office occupied by the Battery Clerk, Bombardier '*Joe*' Dove.

On the occasion of one of the Pay Parades the money, mostly in five franc notes, having been drawn by an officer from the Field Cashier, was issued to the personnel on the Battery position. Then it was Joe's duty to take the remainder back to the Wagon Line to pay the drivers and others stationed there.

Now Joe was more at home in an office chair than in a saddle and when a mount was brought up for him, it was so anxious

to get back to its friends at the Wagon Line that it set off at a gallup before Joe could get his right leg over the saddle and find the stirrup. Clinging on for dear life Joe disappeared in a cloud of dust and five franc notes and we could only hope that there would be enough money left to pay the waiting drivers.

At the back of the main building was a barn under a large walnut tree and behind this a tiny garden plot with a small lean-to shed in one corner in which three

The Battery Clerk wasn't really at home on a horse

other signallers and myself took up our quarters. Growing over the side and roof was a vine bearing very small grapes which were very sweet and didn't last long.

The cookhouse was established round the corner and one of the cooks had adopted a small fox terrier pup called 'Bulger' which used to wake us in the morning by tearing round to our shed and chewing any part of us which happened to be protruding from the blankets.

The telephone line to the O.P. had to be patrolled each day and the O.P. manned every night, a duty which came round every second or third day. We elected to check the line in the early morning as this was the quietest part of the day and it was not unpleasant to set off about 4 or 5 o'clock on the tour.

It was a hot summer and several of us sent home for khaki shorts which were more comfortable than breeches. I had

The line had to be looped high up away from the nightly traffic of limbers and ambulances

also sent home for some gum boots which were invaluable for our walk through the long dew-soaked grass. Passing the Battery, asleep except for the solitary guard, we followed the thin telephone line through the wood, along a hedge skirting a large moat-surrounded farm and onto the road leading down to the trenches.

Along this stretch the line had to be looped high up between the trees away from the nightly traffic of limbers and ambulances. Soon the road approached a railway level crossing — no danger of trains here — but just before reaching it a lane labelled *Cheapside* branched off to the left and a little way along here we had a second O.P. in a cottage. A large walnut tree grew in the garden from which, later in the autumn, we collected pounds and pounds of nuts and very nice they were too.

The stretch of road beyond the level crossing was unsafe to use in daylight being in full view of the German trenches and movement on it was apt to attract the unwelcome attentions of a machine gun. Instead of following the road we crossed the rails about 100 yards to the right and through the yard of Wagon Farm where a most appalling smell advertised the presence of a mule or cow which had been dead for a very long time.

Beyond this point we crept round hedges until we reached the O.P. which was a wooden shed standing in the corner of a field bordering the road from Ypres to the village of Boesinghe lying just on our left. It was at this point that the huge loop of the Ypres Salient came round to join the north-south line of trenches held at this time by the French and Belgians and stretched up to the coast. Beyond the drained bed of the Yser canal which lay just across the road in front of us was the tumbled area of trenches on an almost imperceptible slope up to Langemark, held by the Germans whose defensive positions always seemed to overlook ours.

To the right of the O.P. a number of cottages lined the road and it was interesting to explore these; this could only be done on a misty day as they were visible by the enemy and all unnecessary movement near the O.P. was naturally forbidden.

Our route of exploration led through a hedge into the garden of the first cottage where the currants still growing there were soon disposed of. The buildings were badly damaged by shell fire and in the upper rooms the windows commanding a view of the canal had been hurriedly barricaded. Everywhere were ample signs of resistance during the retreat in the early days of the war in the form of French cartridge cases, bayonets and pieces of equipment. It was a sad sight to see the contents of drawers tumbled out on the floor and one turned over these pathetic fragments in search of some small souvenir with a feeling of guilt and sorrow for the inhabitants who had been forced to leave their home in hurried flight. I picked up a small photograph of a charming old lady in a lace cap trimmed with black ribbon which had been taken by a photographer in the Rue aux Beurre, Ypres.

A smell of damp plaster and brick dust pervaded the scene and at dusk the silence became even more haunting and menacing. As daylight faded countless frogs in the ponds and ditches set up their melancholy croaking. The rise and fall of verey lights caused the shadows of broken buildings to move silently across the brightly illuminated ground and occasional rifle shots gave evidence of watchful life in the seemingly deserted landscape.

The next building was a rather longer one with a range of outhouses behind separated by a paved yard and this had belonged to somebody who had dealt in or repaired bicycles. Scattered about one of the rooms were hundreds of cycle parts but, much to our disappointment, there was nothing like a whole machine. We didn't explore beyond this point as the next building was some distance across the open.

One evening I started out for a *mooch around*. In the haunted silence of those deserted dwellings I passed the first cottage and had just reached the centre of the paved yard when I heard stealthy footsteps. Rooted to the spot with terror I waited in an agony of suspense to see what would come through the open door of one of the outhouses from which the sound seemed to come.

We never carried arms on our visits to the O.P.s or even to the front line and I stood there with prickling scalp expecting to see one of the concealed snipers emerge to start his nightly work, having already experienced these men in our last position.

Nearer and nearer to the door crept the footsteps and then, as the complete anti-climax, there staggered out a weak and emaciated calf which tottered off round the corner. My relief was so great that I never thought of trying to do something for the poor thing as I made my way back to the O.P.

This O.P. was used until September when a shell hit the aperture killing Captain Benn who was observing through it at the time. Captain Benn was very popular with everybody and his untimely death was a sad loss to the Battery. We buried him at Talana Farm which was quite near and one of the official war cemeteries. I had my first leave of five days soon after and I was given the sad task of taking his personal effects to his home in Burley.

What a strange experience that leave was; strange in that all the familiar places seemed so different — it was, of course, I who had changed. One day spent in travelling home and another for the return journey left a mere three days into which to pack so much. Messages from my friends to their families took part of the time and the rest was just being at home with its comforts and joys. Sitting in easy chairs gave one the sensation of falling, so used had we become to *'hard lying'*. Friends and relations flocked round and I felt quite the little hero in my war-stained uniform and cap with the shell splinter hole through it.

The O.P. was now moved back to the cottage with the walnut tree; the targets we fired on so regularly were mostly strong points in farms and the names Farm 14, Fortin 17, Blanc Maison and Krupp Farm, etc., became familiar after such constant use for six months in signal messages. It was surprising to see, on a visit to this district after the war, how all these farms had been rebuilt on their old foundations and seemed to belie our memories of the shattered piles of bricks we had known.

Occasional visits were made to the front and support lines in the Salient to observe special shoots and we were always glad to get away from this scene of desolation; glad too when we had safely passed over one or other of the many rickety duckboard bridges over the muddy canal bed. One never knew when shrapnel or *'Black Marias'* – those beastly high explosive air bursts which exploded with such a venomous crump – would be directed at these tenuous links with the front line.

One day several of us went over into the French sector on our left to visit a battery of 95mm guns which looked as ancient as our own 5 inch howitzers. The gunners had made a home for themselves with little hutments furnished with beds and seats outside made from saplings — all very quaint and rustic. Wooden footways linked gun pits to shelters and were covered overhead with brushwood on poles.

Those with a mechanical turn of mind were busy making souvenirs of rings and paper knives from aluminium fuses and shell cases.

One of the gunners was a photographer who took a picture of the four of us in which one of the group, Albert Vallender, appears to be wearing a sort of miniature apron from the back of his cap. Now whether some army contractor had been particularly persuasive or some A.D.Q.M.G. had slipped up over the destination of our division or whether the

Endless entertainment and a source of amazement

midsummer heat of north Europe had been grossly over-rated is not known but we had been issued with these ridiculous things to protect the neck from sunstroke.

The Battery had been presented with a gramophone by the late Commanding Officer of the Brigade, Colonel W. Stopham Dawson, and this provided endless entertainment in the billets and was a source of amazement to old 'Hookna-Harkna' who apparently had never seen nor heard one before.

One day the old man and his sons appeared as our tiny shed armed with picks and spades and started a long excited harangue which was completely incomprehensible to us but eventually we gathered that he wanted to dig up the earthen floor where we slept. We took a dim view of this but after all it was his property so we moved our stuff out of the way and left them to it.

They unearthed a huge wooden chest full of treasured household belongings which they had buried when the advancing German army had got dangerously near and now that the fighting appeared

Retrieving buried treasure

to have settled down into the stalemate of trench warfare they evidently thought the time was opportune for retrieving their buried treasure.

It seems likely that a visit to Ypres by several of us must have been an unofficial one as I cannot imagine that we could have been sent there on any legitimate business. It just seemed important that we should pay a visit to this notorious place which lay almost within sight of us. Later in the war it became a place to avoid at all costs.

The approach took us down a wide suburban street lined with three and four storeyed houses of which some had lost their outer walls to the action of heavy shells leaving the rooms exposed to view with beds and furniture teetering on the brink of dipping floors. We made our way to the Grande Place and looked at the badly damaged church and the Cloth Hall. In the open arcade at the back of the latter were several old state coaches and vehicles which were soon to be reduced to ashes by the constant bombardment over the years. No shells fell near us while we were there but the ever present threat kept our eyes pricked — it was rather like a grim game of '*musical chairs*' as we lingered past the sheltered places on our route and then hurried over the more exposed parts waiting for the music not to stop but to start.

After the old man at the billet had ruined our shelter by digging up the earth floor we had to find some other accommodation and discovered a little empty room in the next cottage in which an old man we called *Piers* lived by himself.

A novel feature of some of these Belgian cottages was a tiny room reached by a short flight of steps constructed on a sloping trap door which, when opened, gave access to a cellar beneath.

We used the old man's kitchen for cooking our meals and to eat them we sat on chairs at the table which was a distinct advance towards more gracious living.

As *Fritz* seemed to be getting increasingly active a dugout was built at the end of this cottage and on several occasions we had to retire to it; nerve racking moments too when we had to help old Piers, who could only totter about, out of his room then half way along the outside of the building, through a passage to the other side and along the second half to the narrow door of the shelter. Having been urged and pushed as far as that, the old man invariably stopped and turned in the safety of the entrance regardless of his helpers shut out in the open striving frenziedly to get out of reach of those screaming shells.

The insulated telephone wire, of which we laid so many miles, was delivered to us on large wooden drums from which it had to be laboriously transferred to smaller drums of a size capable of being carried on a bar by two men and unwound as the line was laid.

Another type was a small zinc reel which fitted on a spindle projecting from a leather belt but this was far too small and had to be discarded.

Wire always seemed to possess a diabolical life of its own. achieving its most complicated tangles in the most inconvenient places. Most of the early methods of laying lines were sooner or later found to be, if not entirely unworkable, at least unacceptable to us. Whenever possible we preferred to avoid the wires of other units and laid ours over the open ground where they stood a better chance of escaping breakages by human traffic in the dark and where it was easier to spot possible breaks near new shell

Proposed method for transferring wire to smaller drums.

holes. This voluntary isolation was not always practicable and sometimes the line had to be pegged to the wall of a communication trench with all the other wires and then the business of identifying our broken ends amongst perhaps several dozen different lines, all broken by the same shell, became well nigh untolerable.

During nearly six months in this position life settled down into a regular routine and was not without its lighter moments.

A small switchboard in the telephone dugout enabled calls from Brigade, Divisional and Corps H.Q. to be put through to the officers mess and on one occasion while Trumpeter Whitaker was on duty the General Officer Commanding Royal Artillery wished to speak to Major Petrie. The correct procedure, of course, was to contact our O.C. and then inform the H.Q. operator that he was on the line. Having got the Major the unfortunate 'Trump' called up H.Q. saying to whom he thought was the operator 'Here's Major Petrie, put the old b----- on'. Unfortunately the old b—— was already on and in due course poor "Trump" was adequately dealt with.

Our sector of the front was that through which the Germans had broken earlier in the year when they used chlorine gas for the first time and we were haunted by the ever present threat of a repetition.

The first primitive gas masks issued to us consisted of a pad of cotton gauze and flannel on a wire frame on which we were expected to urinate and tie with tapes over our mouth and nose. These were replaced by flannel hoods fitted with goggles which steamed up in use and a mouthpiece having a rubber valve outside which closed when one tried to take a breath through the mouth but opened with a horrible fluttering sound when breathing out. It required quite an effort to draw in sufficient air through the flannel which was impregnated with some sort of chemical making it damp and clammy to the neck where it was tucked in under the tunic collar. It was carried round everywhere in a canvas

'Here's Major Petrie, put the old b..... on'

satchel and it certainly proved its usefulness when the Germans made another gas attack on December 19th.

In the cold dark hour before dawn on that day we four in the tiny room of old Pier's cottage were wakened up by a terrific bombardment of the trenches. As soon as the shutters were opened my throat was caught by the choking vapour which was curling about outside. '*This is it*' I thought and the first panic reaction was to take to my heels anywhere to get away from this evil insidious cloud which crept slowly and silently over the ground with the slight movement of wind.

My cry of '*Gas*' brought the others from their beds and then followed a feverish hunt for gas masks. Mine did not appear to be in the room but with the aid of a torch I found it hanging on a coat hook outside in the passage. Pulling the foul thing on I buttoned up my tunic to enclose the skirts of the hood and pushed the mouthpiece into my mouth. It was horrible not being able to suck in any air through that and I thought I would never be able to breathe through the thick flannel but eventually I found that the thing worked and we made our way to the other side of the building where the off-duty N.C.O.s had gathered. It was like some ghastly nightmare to see these inhuman figures moving about; instead of the familiar faces there were only horrible impersonal masks with sightless goggle eyes in the dim light of two or three candles which flickered in the incessant cannonade going on outside. To add to the despondency one of the nameless figures gave an agonised cry '*My God, I can't breathe!*' and knowing just how he felt we helped him to adjust his respirator and take it easy.

The explosions outside were now swelled by the Battery which had been roused by the guard and was firing on its S.O.S. lines to such purpose that, as later ascertained, the attacking Germans had been pulverised as they left their trenches and what was left of our infantry were able to deal with the rest of them.

Presently dawn came in a clear sky and going outside we cautiously tested the air; the gas cloud appeared to have passed and we thankfully removed our respirators and gulped in the clear air which had never tasted so sweet.

Now we had to get busy restoring communications with the O.P. and we were working on these for the rest of the morning while the shelling gradually died down and we were able to break off for a long delayed breakfast.

It was a long time before we even thought of what might have happened to the old Belgian. His little room was always closely shuttered and apparently he had put his head under the blankets and escaped any ill effects.

The guard at the Battery had delayed putting on his gas mask until he had roused the gunners to action and suffered from the effects of the gas. So also had some of the gun crews who found it impossible to lay the sun sights through their steamed up goggles and these casualties were sent down to the wagon line.

Ammunition for our antiquated weapons was very short and during our six months occupation of this position, firing was kept to the minimum. There were times when replacement of shells fired during the day could be effected by bringing them up with the rations and mail in the mess cart. Compared with future occasions when our new 4.5 inch

Our linesman's billet at Brielen

weapons would often fire many hundreds of rounds in a single night this situation in 1915 was ludicrous. After such an unusual expenditure of ammunition on December 19th all available wagon teams had to be brought up to the Battery in broad daylight. Such activity naturally drew retaliation from the Germans but fortunately all the wagons were able to unload and get away without casualties.

This vicious attack put an end to what had been a comparatively comfortable period and for the rest of that month when at last we were relieved by another division our nerves were on edge and an atmosphere of tension affected everybody. Several men were wounded by shells which dropped round the billet which had been our home from July to December, and the strain of being exposed for such a long period to enemy action now began to make itself felt. It was a most welcome relief when the Battery pulled out and our anxieties diminished as the distance from the front line increased.

1916: *Preparing for the Somme Offensive*

'Practising our schoolboy French'

January 4

OUT OF ACTION at last, the New Year found us billeted in various farms and cottages about 5 kilometres from Arneke, B subsection being allotted to a large barn belonging to a farm at the end of a narrow lane.

It wasn't long before my friend Ray Renwick had established good relations with the farmer and his family called *Declerck* who invited us in for coffee in the evenings and we were able to practice our schoolboy French.

Two delightful little girls aged about 9 and 10 made much of us and when we left the district four weeks later I was presented with a small card decorated with birds and flowers and inscribed with the words, '*De loin comme de pres je pense à vous, souvenir de ta petite amie Marie Declerck*' — which still reminds me of one of the happiest periods of the whole war.

The signallers had an easy time on telephone duty at the sergeants mess where we were comfortably installed in the kitchen of the local blacksmith. Coffee was always available through the night and with no turning out to mend broken lines we were in clover.

January 10

The Battery Staff took part in a number of exercises which were thoroughly enjoyable as they involved a lot of riding about the countryside. One of the most comfortable mounts I ever had was a neat little chestnut mare called '*Dolly*' which died mysteriously during the night. It had an easy action and perfect disposition and was eagerly sought after by several NCOs.

It was here that a young dog, which came to be known as '*Darky*'[1], attached itself to the Battery. It was in poor condition but was carefully restored to health by Driver C. Howitt.

January 12
The estaminets and shops in Arneke were a popular attraction in the evenings and it was on my way there with several others that we met Sergeant Gee, the No. 1 of B subsection, who handed me a gold printed card of commendation from the G.O.C.R.A. General Percival on my work on December 19th. This was all very pleasing and completely unexpected and I bought myself a wrist watch for about £2 on the strength of it.

January 17
Jack Boden, the very popular No. 1 of A subsection, and a local bank manager before joining up, left us to train for a commission and was given a good send off.

January 22
Guard duty on the gun park came round quite often as leave passes were coming through fairly quickly which left the Battery rather short handed. It was during my second turn of duty that I was visited by Reg Rhodes, another signaller, who told me that we had both been awarded the DCM for our work during the gas attack on December 19th. I was completely taken aback and rather overwhelmed as I couldn't imagine that what we did was more than we came out to do.

January 23
Reg Rhodes and I, together with Percy King who had been awarded the MM, were instructed to prepare ourselves to go to an unspecified destination to receive our decorations. The mess cart took us to Esquelbecque where a London Transport bus was waiting to take us with others to a field near Hazebrouck — here we were joined by about 30 or 40 officers, NCOs and men who were to have their medal ribbons pinned on by General Plumer.

It was quite an occasion with a number of '*brasshats*' present and a large band which played suitable music while the General moved slowly down the line. He spoke to each man as he pinned on the appropriate ribbon after the citation had been read out by an attendant staff officer. After the parade and march past the bus took us back to Esquelbecque where we three marked the occasion by having a good meal at a restaurant before walking back the few kilometres to Arneke.

January 24
The Battery Staff practised coming into action several times during the morning

---

[1] This little dog became the Battery mascot and stayed with us till the end of the war when unfortunately it was not allowed to be brought back to England and, sadly, had to be destroyed. It loved to be with the horses at the wagon lines and always accompanied the ammunition wagons on their journeys up to the Battery positions and it was on one of these trips to Nieuport in 1917 that it was wounded in the leg.

and it just happened that the second OP was in a very nice estaminet in Bolleezeele at a convenient time for coffee.

January 25
All the old ammunition was stowed in the wagons ready to be taken away to the Divisional Ammunition Column as the new 4.5 inch howitzers which were to replace our old 5 inch relics were waiting to be collected at the railhead.

January 26
The new guns were eagerly inspected by everybody and this, of course, meant that we were due for a lot of hard work in learning to operate these effective little weapons.

I helped Wilf Dawson and Jim Turner to make a small scale model landscape for the officers to practise ranging on targets. It was good fun and we felt like kids on the sands making houses out of match boxes and roads out of strips of white cloth etc.

The signallers tried out some new signalling lamps which gave good results up to 1000 yards.

January 29
Was persuaded to play in a rugger match between the sections (RX comprising A and B guns, LX being C and D guns). It was a wild rough and tumble affair and I felt very stiff afterwards.

This was followed next day by a match between the Brigade officers and men in which the Medical Officer dislocated his leg. Most of the officers are very keen players, Captain Eddison being of international standard.

February 3 — 11
Inevitably our stay in these pleasant surroundings came to an end and after saying goodbye to the Declercks and all those who had been so kind to us we left the gun park at 3.30 and hauled our new guns and wagons to the railway at Bavinchove.

Entraining vehicles and horses went smoothly enough and we left soon after 10.00 pm but the carriages were horribly uncomfortable and we crawled through the night with many stops.

Passing through St. Omer, Abbeville, Calais and Boulogne we detrained at a station a few kilometres past Amiens about 11.00 o'clock next morning.

Taking to the road again we travelled back through Amiens which impressed us as a fine town with its wide streets and large shops crowded with people. Several times we caught a glimpse of the sea and our thoughts turned with longing to what lay beyond the Channel.

Our billet for the night was a burnt out chateau with extensive stables which we shared with the horses. Next morning we moved on to La Chaussee Tirancourt, a small village in lovely hilly country overlooking the Somme valley across which lies Picquiney, another pleasant village about a kilometre away.

Gun Park
Cavaplas

The gun park was on the open hillside above the village from where we could just see Amiens in the distance. The horses had to be watered down in the valley where the river spread rather wide over the flat marshy edges. When riding one horse bareback and leading another one had to lean well back on entering the water to avoid being thrown over the horse's head as its front legs sank in the mud and its head went down to drink.

Poor old Archer, a signaller, was rather unfortunate on his first trip and took a header into the water which was colder than he would have liked as it had been snowing all night. The horses were very fresh and lively and on these occasions, the halter rope had to be tied round the animal's nose for extra control; at mid-day 'Stables', when they were being walked round and round for exercise nearly 40 men, including myself, had their names taken and were given extra guard and picket duties.

February 14
The morning was cold and wet as we left La Chaussee and moved on through Vignacourt to Villars Bocage which was a drab dirty place containing a number of tumbledown cottages in which we were billetted. The horses were picketted in an orchard, the vehicles being parked on the road side and here I spent a miserable night doing my extra guard duty.

Fortunately we left this filthy place next morning and marched through Molliens-au Bois and Contay to Warloy where the billets were in barns fitted with wire netting bunks in tiers. Here we discovered a well stocked *Expeditionary Force Canteen* which helped to add to our comfort.

The weather continued cold and wet and our signalling practice was often carried out in a cottage where we were able to buy coffee amongst a menagerie of cats, dogs and small children.

The lady of the house looked thin and pinched but was extremely kind. She showed us a photograph of her brother who had been killed in the Champagne sector. We found another cottage where coffee was available and where the two daughters made a poor living weaving the material and making cardigan jackets; they were paid only one franc for making up each garment taking almost a full day to make one.

February 19
In one of my letters from home I was told that my brother Stanley was said to be stationed at Naours with his ASC unit and as this was within reasonable distance I obtained permission to visit him. Passing through Baiseux and Corbie I reached Naours to find that he had left about a fortnight ago and was thought to be at Pont Noyelles about 4 kilometres away and it was here that I found him. After giving my horse a feed I had a meal with him in his lorry and a very pleasant talk and exchange of news before setting off on my return journey.

The weather turned cold and frosty with plenty of snow but our cottage provided a warm retreat and the days passed quite pleasantly with occasional guard duties at the gun park which was a huge steel shed with a concrete floor, probably a cattle market.

The guard room, so called, was a small space surrounded by hessian screens to keep off the icy wind and a fire bucket.

February 25
During the night this sacking caught fire and in seconds there was quite a blaze. We were forced to manhandle the ammunition wagons as far away as possible to prevent the shells and charges in them from blowing up. The alarm was raised and the gunners and drivers came streaming up the road from their billets but by this time the fire had burnt itself

out together with most of our kit, several sets of harness and a rifle.

February 26
I developed a heavy cold and felt pretty miserable for several days. The cold wet days of early February had turned to snow and frost but now a thaw had set in and I found that the warmest place was the telephone room where I put in some hours of duty.

A visit to the local hall where the Royal Garrison Artillery were giving a concert passed an hour or two in the evening. One or two turns were quite good but the piano badly needed tuning and must have given the pianist an unhappy time — as it did to the audience.

Gunfire could be heard in the distance and there was a constant movement at night of heavy guns and ammunition convoys passing through the village towards the front.

As the days dragged on my condition showed no improvement and I felt as weak as a kitten. Having no faith in the young MO I didn't report sick and spent two days in bed but my wire netting bunk in the dark draughty barn was not conducive to a quick recovery.

One day I crept out to a neighbouring cottage to get a shave but the barber's razor must have been very blunt as it was an agonising experience.

There was talk of a move being imminent so I thought that it would be better if I was up on my feet and pottered about in the telephone room.

March 4
We left Warloy in a snowstorm but moved only a few kilometres to Contay where the streets were named after those in Leeds; our billet was in Boar Lane, an

Billets for 120 men   *Cookhouse for 120 men*

Author's note

1916–1917
Clarification of the chapter headings

MOST PEOPLE know that *The Somme* was one of the big offensives of World War I and started on July 1st 1916. But where did it take place, how long did it last and when did it end?

FOR THOSE who were there, it was just another attempt to break through the static trench system. The whole battlefield – including the French sector south of the River Somme – extended for more than 20 miles. The northern sectors, in the region of the River Ancre, faced enormously strong German positions on higher ground and the men of the *New Army* suffered very heavy casualties with little gain. South of Albert, the Germans were less prepared and both the British and French achieved limited success. There followed many costly engagements which dragged on month after month into December and finally petered out as another year of war approached.

THE APPARENT LACK of any real success, plus the horrifying casualty lists over the past three years, reduced British morale to its lowest ebb. It was even rumoured that mutiny had broken out in the French Army and we ourselves were dangerously close. Our faith in the ability of our commanders to break the stalemate of trench warfare was shattered and, utterly exhausted mentally and physically, we faced the year 1917 in deep dejection.

Norman Tennant

earth floored barn behind the village street. Feeling like death warmed up, but only slightly, I stayed in bed next day where I was discovered by the OC on his tour of inspection. He sent the MO to see me, who, as expected gave me some pills and told me to attend sick parade next morning. More pills and *'light duty'* so I collected my bridle and bit to clean. After several days of creeping about doing odd jobs I spotted a couple of big rats in the muddy ditch below the billet; loading my rifle I bagged one with the second shot but the noise was so startling in that quiet village that I gave it up and hastily cleaned the rifle barrel again.

March 8
Feeling rather better I borrowed one of the Battery cycles and rode to Warloy to pick up my bandolier which my brother had left at the EF Canteen for me; apparently I'd forgotten it when I went to see him at Pont Noyelles. I returned by way of Baizeuz and Franvillers to find that he had called at my billet in my absence, leaving a message to say that he was now stationed at Herissart about 5 kilometres away.

March 9
We practised for some mounted sports including such events as bareback wrestling, tug of war, VC races etc. The horses were rather fresh and frisky and several injuries occurred.

Billets for three officers, chargers and two dogs

Billets for three officers

March 11
On the last turn of guard from 4 to 6 a.m. in the gun park which is in a tree lined square with the Mairie at one end and a church at the other. While sheltering in the church porch I got into conversation with a French *poilu* from Bordeaux who was also on guard over something, I don't know what.

March 12
The officers were billetted in a small chateau and today being Sunday a church parade was held in the grounds. In the afternoon I walked 5 kilometres to Herissart only to find that my brother was out somewhere with his lorry. I waited until he returned about 4.30 and we had tea together.

March 13
In a shop in the village I saw some large tins up on a shelf; the labels were only partly visible but the letters *POI* . . suggested that they contained pears. I bought two without further examination and found after I got back to the billet that the part of the label I had failed to see contained one letter *S* instead of the three . . . *RES* which I had expected so instead of the nice juicy *POIRES* I had been looking forward to I had a large quantity of *POIS* which I didn't want.

March 15
The Battery received sudden orders to move but only as far as the next village Beaucourt sur l'Hallue. After watering and feeding we had to move again and retraced our steps through Contay to Harponville where we found a snug little room with three beds which I shared with Jim Turner and Frank Keighley.

March 18
After tea Jim and I walked over to our little cottage at Warloy and were followed soon after by Arthur Driver. We were made welcome, given coffee and after a pleasant evening we walked back to Harponville in brilliant moonlight.

March 19th
Percy King was celebrating his birthday with a number of parcels from home and his parcels were quite something to write home about. Chicken in aspic, fruit salad and cakes etc., helped to sweeten my guard duty that night.

March 22
Jack Boden sent me a copy of the *Daily Sketch* which had printed four of my allegedly humorous drawings and my photograph on the two centre pages.

March 29
We left Harponville just as a battalion of infantry who were to take over our billets entered the other end of the village. A sunny morning helped to improve the drabness of Villers Bocage where we stopped to water and feed before moving on thankfully to Canaples. The fine spell was of short duration and we moved through several heavy snowstorms. The new horse lines and gun parks of the two howitzer batteries were together in a

huge field alongside the railway on which a heavy traffic of troop trains passed each day. The watering troughs were filled from a stream by a steam pump which was a welcome relief for the gunners who often have to pass the canvas buckets from hand to hand in a long line.

April 1
Ray celebrated his birthday today and having discovered a nice little house with a spare room just outside the village, he invited eleven of his friends to a party to share the contents of twelve parcels which he had received from home. He had borrowed the Battery gramophone and we all enjoyed the evening.

An enjoyable birthday

April 2
The weather had now turned warm and sunny and as it was Sunday we played our sister battery at soccer but lost 2-1. The traditional rivalry between Otley and Ilkley must have resulted in some rough play as one man in the opposing team had his arm broken.

April 16
I received a copy of *The Buzzer* for March containing one of my sketches; this is a small magazine produced by the 49th Division to which I contributed some drawings.

April 22
The fine weather has broken and we are getting a lot of rain. On guard again and we all cursed the Orderly Officer, Lieutenant Douglas (known as '*The Wemmil*') when he turned out the guard in a heavy downpour to enquire if all was well.

April 24
The OC took me with him to Berteaucourt, about 15 kilometres away, to collect a map of which he wanted me to make a copy. As this was not available he sent me back while he made a further search. After dinner the map arrived and I got busy on it and managed to finish it about 9.30 pm.

April 25
The Battery Staff turned out for a field day with the infantry; from our OP in an old windmill we could see them advancing in open order across the fields. Some were carrying the new Lewis guns which I think were a recent issue.

April 28
Our first ration of lime juice was issued today — very nice but strong and needed diluting. The men were being innoculated in batches with anti-tetanus serum; this meant 24 hours off duty and owing to this and the number of leave passes coming through there was an acute shortage of men. In fact B subsection could only muster 3 men to water and feed 16 horses.

May 1
The days passed with field exercises, telephone and guard duty, signalling practice, football matches, reading and swimming in the wood, harness cleaning and always there were the horses to groom, water and feed and exercise. Four of us walked the five kilometres to Vignacourt to a show given by the 49th Division concert part, '*The Tykes*'. Half the Battery seems to be sleeping out in various kinds of shelters now that the weather has turned warmer. Ray, with his gift for organising things, has produced a tent from somewhere which we erected in the wood.

May 3
My thoughts turned to home affairs as my mother was putting on a show in the town hall tonight in aid of the hospital in which she worked. She had trained a number of local children to act in a short play and perform a few turns.

May 4
Was detailed to act as horse holder to Sergeant Gee and Corporal Dawson who went to a training camp for officers and NCOs in the district. We watched a crack battery of the Royal Horse Artillery come into action and do some fancy driving though I couldn't imagine our *heavy-wheelers* emulating the light draught animals of the RHA tearing about with their 13 pounder guns.

My turn for innoculation after tea. Had a surprise visitor in the form of Teddy Ledger, an old Ilkley Grammar

School boy who was stationed at Naours with the 6th Duke of Wellingtons.

May 6
About 9 o'clock at night a very excited Frenchman rushed into the billet to say, we gathered, that his horse had fallen down the bank into the stream; we turned out with torches and managed to effect a rescue.

May 9
Another Battery Staff exercise in which Percy King acted as Forward Observation Officer. Our OP was a haystack.

May 14
All the horses in the Battery are being reshuffled so that one subsection has all black, another has all chestnut and another has all bay, etc. The ammunition is being broken up and the horses and men divided between the batteries.

A large barn in the village is being converted into a cinema by the Divisional REs and is naturally called the White Rose Cinema as the divisional emblem is a white Tudor rose.

Lieutenant Whitaker returned from his 7 days leave yesterday and today he received orders to go to London to be decorated with the M.C. Lucky man! Perfect timing!

May 17
A very grand horse show was organised with individual and team races. It was held in a large field surrounded by woods; the weather was perfect and the crowds milling round the numerous marquees to the stirring music of the Divisional band brought a touch of peacetime festivities.

Our training during the early months of 1916 was in preparation for what became known as *The Somme Offensive*. Of course we had no knowledge of any such plans and simply carried out our daily exercises quite happy to be away from the front. Just why we had to move so frequently from one village to another in the area east of Amiens we never knew nor cared but supposed there must have been some good reason. As May gave place to June our exercises become merged with other units in more complicated manoeuvres and we gradually became aware of impending events of a more serious nature.

May 20
Regretfully we said goodbye to Canaples where we had been since March 28th and moved to join the rest of the Brigade at Pernois where a deeper feeling of urgency attended our training. The days were filled with Brigade Manoeuvres, Battery Staff exercises, medical inspections and ceremonial guard mounting, etc.

While out grazing the horses we came across some trench mortars, a new weapon to us. We could see the large bomb like a football travel through the air and land in a dummy trench to explode like an 8 inch shell.

Oo said 'Happy birthday'

June 2–4

Reveille at 3.30 and the Battery moved off in pursuit of an opposing force, coming into action when they were located. We spent the night in the field near Canaples where the horse show was held in May, lit a fire on the edge of a wood and prepared the first meal we had eaten since breakfast at 5 am.

At 3.30 next morning we saddled up and were away in twenty minutes. This time we were supposed to be retiring and after coming into action several times we returned to Pernois to water and feed the horses and have a belated breakfast.

Somewhere during the last two days I had lost my diary and next day, being Sunday, I obtained permission to go and look for it as I had an idea where it might be. Fortunately I was right and there it was on the ground where we had established an OP in one of our actions; I had used it to jot down range corrections to signal back to the Battery.

June 5–10

My 20th birthday — on guard — rain, rain — cold — misery! To complete the depression I came off duty to find that all my friends had gone off to the White Rose Cinema at Canaples.

More mounted exercises, mostly in the rain. More frequent guard duty due to extreme shortage of men — still raining day after sodden day. Flaming June!

June 11

Reveille at 3.30 and we left Pernois for Senlis which is packed with troops, mostly Scottish, who are wearing the new steel helmets. We thought they looked rather silly, the helmets not the troops.

June 14–18

Went up to the gun position with four other signallers in the mess cart, wearing the *'tin hats'* with which we too had been issued.

The country here is well wooded and hilly and quite different from the flat Belgian landscape that we had so far been in.

The whole area is alive with men working on gun pits, dugouts and trenches without any apparent attempt at concealment from aerial observation. The space allotted to us lies between the road from Aveloy to Authuille and the river Ancre which flows along the edge of Martinsart Wood just behind us. In front the ground rises gently towards Authuille Wood and the valley beyond where the front line is overlooked by the strong German defences round Thiepval.

The gun pits and dugouts had already been constructed by fatigue parties and now our job was to establish telephone communication with Brigade HQ several OPs and the officers mess which, together with the cookhouse, are situated a little way up Blighty Valley across the road.

The guns arrived between 4 and 5 pm. on the 15th and were pushed into their emplacements. RE signals turned up with some large drums of armoured cable (so called) which had to be buried in 6 foot trenches.

June 19
It was while digging one of these that the value of our new steel helmets was very clearly demonstrated. Just as Jim was bringing his pickaxe down Arthur suddenly bent forward in the trench and there was a nasty clang as it hit Arthur's tin hat. It could easily have been curtains for Arthur!

June 20
Arthur and I discovered an abandoned RE pontoon in the flooded low ground of Martinsart Wood beyond the river and we spent a pleasant evening poling it about in a rather erratic course between the trees.

June 21 & 22
Visits to the OPs come fairly frequently as the guns have to be registered on a number of different targets but some are too distant to be seen from the ground and have to be spotted by an observer from a plane. For this purpose a Royal Flying Corps wireless operator was temporarily attached to the Battery to receive the range corrections but messages from ground to plane had to be sent in code by means of white linen strips laid on the ground to form letters.

Our chief pleasure here is bathing in the Ancre which flows gently past about 50 yards behind the line of gun pits and dugouts. The river is only 6 feet wide and what a delight it is on these hot days to swim upsteam a little way and then float down with the current hidden from a mad world by the high bank on one side

A rather erratic course between the trees

and Martinsart Wood on the other.

German planes are very active watching our preparations and we saw several fights as our machines arrived to drive off the intruders.

June 23
Cycled with Frank Keighley to Brigade HQ in Albert to collect some telephone equipment and took the opportunity to look round the town with its famous leaning gilded figure of the Madonna on the basilica tower and to buy as much canteen foodstuffs as we could carry.

One of our observation balloons broke loose in a heavy thunder storm and disappeared in the direction of Germany.

June 24
Spent the day with Frank and an officer to observe the start of the preliminary bombardment from No. 19 OP which was constructed in a sap off, a communication trench called Pendle Hill Street. A certain amount of retaliatory fire fell round the OP as was to be expected since the Germans had had ample time to register accurately every trench and dugout so blatantly advertised. We returned through a communication trench which wound its way down the inside edge of Blighty Wood; cut into the solid chalk its twists and turns and the trees growing above restricted one's vision to a few yards and one felt so safe.

June 25
Spent the morning working the ground-to-plane signal strips which are 12 feet long by 1 foot wide. We also rigged up a red disc in front of the gun pits which could be changed to white by means of a wire from the signal dugout when the Battery was required to fire salvoes. The heavy bombardment continues all day.

June 26
All day at the OP with Lieut. Holmes. About 2.15 a cloud of gas was released from our front line on the left, followed by another at 5'o'clock to which the *Boches* replied with heavy mortar fire round the OP. The communication trench outside was badly knocked about and we returned by a detour via Crucifix Corner, a road junction half way between the Battery and Aveloy.

June 27
Accompanied Frank and the Major to an OP in the wood behind us near Mesnil. A huge tree had been fitted with a ladder and observation platform from which there was an extensive view of the German lines covered with an almost continuous inferno of smoke and flame from bursting shells of all calibres. Our target was a machine gun emplacement on which the Battery scored a number of direct hits.

June 28
Today exposed the futility of laying every unit's armoured cable under the duckboards in the bottom of the communication trenches. One lucky high angle shell or trench mortar was sufficient to sever all the lines which were

merely covered with twisted galvanised wire. This is exactly what happened soon after we reached the OP on the forward slope of Pendle Hill Street and the heavy rain reduced the trench bottom to a mass of sticky mud. The problem of identifying the two ends of our particular cable from the tangle of loose wires and mending them in the constant stream of stretcher bearers, runners and fatigue parties, etc., tried our patience to the utmost and we eventually abandoned the cables in favour of thin rubber insulated lines laid over the open.

June 29

Spent most of the day laying another line to the OP. About 10 p.m. a few shells fell round the gun position, one scattering a pile of empty ammunition boxes, but most exploded harmlessly in the marsh behind.

June 30

OP duty again and the new line was blown to bits and took a long time to repair. The long awaited offensive is due to start tomorrow and we were all prepared to move forward wondering just what this would entail.

For many months past my night-time duties on the telephone had provided an opportunity to make a number of pencil sketches of incidents, both real and imaginary, and caricatures of the men and officers. To pass some of the hours of waiting the Major asked me to let him see these and I took them round to the mess.

The poor duty signaller and Lieutenant Eddison

Impressions...

An experiment in beds

Sketching

MYSELF

The lemonade-monger

The 'Lead-swinger'

'D3' as thin as telephone wire

The Battery 'Anti-Aircraft Section'!

caught in the German barrage and the trench was choked with the bodies of men who had not even got as far as our front line. One of them must have been unusually tall as he looked so pathetically long and thin lying there along the bottom of the trench. It was a relief to get back to the Battery position about 10 p.m.

July 2
The day passed reasonably quietly and a swim in the stream helped to restore morale. At 6 p.m. Percy King and I went down to relieve the others at the OP and to await another attack which is to be made in the morning. I am now sitting with the telephone receiver strapped to my head while the dugout steps fill up with infantry waiting to move into the front line.

July 1
'Z' Day at last and the high hopes we have entertained for so long are being put to the test. The infantry went over the top at 7.30 and were said to have reached the German front line. A few were reported to have got as far as Thiepval but couldn't be supported and were presumably killed or captured.

Conflicting reports seemed to suggest a serious setback on our front relieved by more optimistic ones from further south. The fact that only four very young prisoners were escorted down the road in front added to our gloom and disappointment.

At the OP the day was a harrowing one. Our supporting infantry moving down Pendle Hill Street outside had been

July 3
I think it was the Buffs, West Kents and West Sussex who went over the top at 3 a.m. and got as far as the German second line of trenches but had to retire to our own front line with heavy losses owing to a lack of bombs and ammunition.

Our telephone line was blown to bits and we were busy all day repairing the breaks. We abandoned the OP and moved to another nearby which had already been prepared for use.

July 5
At 2 p.m. Arthur and I were sent with Lieutenant Douglas as contact with the OP had been lost but on arrival we found

that the duty men had just finished laying out a fresh line so we were not required.

The Battery was heavily '*strafed*' with gas shells and HE but although several dugouts were hit there were no casualties apart from streaming eyes from the effects of the gas.

At 5 p.m. the guns suddenly opened a terrific bombardment for 18 minutes in support of another attack which succeeded in capturing the Hindenburg Redoubt which had defied us for so long.

July 6
Down to the OP again at 6.15 a.m. and spent a quiet day until 4 o'clock when our artillery plastered the German trenches for a short time.

Last night Frank Keighley came back with a slight wound in the neck and left us for the dressing station.

July 7
Another attack this morning with very little success.

One of our planes, a BE 2 C flying very low, was brought down by a passing shell from an 18 pounder battery and fell near the cookhouse, both pilot and observer being killed. A pencilled note on a message pad in the cockpit read,

'Can you see all those horses at Miraumont?'

Our medical orderly was wounded by a premature burst from one of our guns.

It rained steadily all day and the swamp creeps nearer and nearer to our dugout entrances.

July 9
All day at the OP from 6 a.m. to 8.15 p.m. Desultory shelling by both sides but at 5.20 we let them have it thick and fast for 25 minutes, then a slight pause to bring the enemy out of their dugouts followed by another storm of shelling for 20 minutes. For a long time after that parties under Red Cross flags were seen to be removing the dead and wounded.

July 10
Some of the men seem to have discovered a new sport; they wade into the swamp and knock fish over the head with a heavy stick — difficult to believe but quite a lot have been caught.

A new sport

July 14–15

Detailed to go with two other signallers and a liaison officer for a 48 hour duty at 7th Battalion West Yorkshire HQ in a captured German trench. Just before dawn the *Boche* attacked with liquid fire and got into our trench but were quickly bombed out again. We managed to pass through the SOS signal to the artillery before our wire went dead.

There was much excitement in the dugout as the officers checked their revolvers to the accompaniment of sharp orders and the constant traffic of runners up and down the steps while the ground shook with the vibration of heavy shells and mortars.

For some reason we never carried arms on our visits to the trenches and we began to feel a little anxious and vulnerable.

The rest of the night we were busy mending the line and after breakfast we laid a new one. Much to our surprise and delight we were relieved about 4 p.m. and wasted no time in getting back to the Battery where everybody had heard that the Germans had got into our trench and thought that we had been taken prisoners.

July 19

While the Battery was engaged in a firing programme this afternoon, 'B' gun had a premature burst which wounded Dick Hornby in the shoulder and ankle and pierced the gun shield in several places.

At this period a number of defective shells, said to be from America, burst as they left the gun muzzle causing too many unnecessary casualties. This additional hazard was unnerving to the gun crews who were ordered to take temporary cover when each round was fired by means of a longer lanyard.

July 23

Albert Vallender and 'Trump' Whitaker rigged up a small weather-cock on the telephone dugout roof so that, when the wind blows in a direction favourable for a German cloud gas attack, it completes a circuit and lights a red lamp inside so that the Battery can be alerted.

These two characters, one tall and thin and the other short, were the subject of many of my sketches and helped to keep us amused with their antics.

July 24

On my way back from the officers mess in *'Blighty Valley'* I was caught by a sudden burst of fire and had to dive behind an old French gun pit while shrapnel and HE shells raised a dust.

Inventors of the 'German Gas Attack Alert System'

July 25

About 10.30 when I was thinking of going for a swim the *Boche* sent a few rounds of shrapnel just over the position and for the next seven hours there was a steady rain of 5.9, 4.2 and gas shells on the Battery. Obviously this was a deliberate attempt to destroy us and it certainly seemed as if the German batteries were going to succeed. 'C' gun had a shell through the roof of the emplacement and was put out of action, 'B' gun had half its shield blown away and several dugouts were hit.

Miraculously there wasn't a single casualty, but everyone's eyes were streaming and aching from the effects of the gas and the place looked a bit of a shambles.

July 26

Many of the shell holes were filled in and 'C' gun pit rebuilt, the gun itself being taken out and sent back to Warloy for replacement. 'B' gun was still usable.

Hundreds of fish are floating about on the surface of the swamp, killed by the concussion of bursting shells in yesterday's strafe. We had fried fish for supper.

July 27

After a trip to the OP to test the line I went for a swim but came out rather hastily as another burst of shelling started. A hostile plane was flying overhead for some time, probably observing the result of the shelling until one of ours came over and shot it down.

July 28

Felt very seedy this morning when I went down to the trenches with the liaison party and as I seemed to get so much worse in the afternoon Lieutenant Butler made me see the infantry MO who promptly sent me back to the dressing station. Calling at the Battery to report and collect some gear I learned that another premature burst from 'A' gun had wounded Gunner Joule.

July 29–August 1

Reached the 2nd Field Ambulance on a stretcher about 5 a.m. and then further back to 44 Casualty Clearing Station where the MO marked me for Base.

The wards are in marquees alongside a branch line where a hospital train is loaded up each day to evacuate the sick and wounded to the Base. It was natural, but very disappointing to me, that more urgent cases should be taken first and as the days went by my hopes for a place dwindled.

Fellow inmates of Lady Hadfields Anglo-American Hospital

August 2–11

At last I was put onto the Red Cross train which moved off to Boulogne where I was taken to Lady Hadfields Anglo-American Hospital at Wimereux. This had been converted from a large hotel in the main street and after a bath I was put into a room containing six beds. What utter joy it was to be lying in clean pyjamas between cool sheets and to be tended by nurses in their spotless uniforms.

My card was marked *PUO*, whatever that meant, and my hopes rose when men with similar labels were sent off to England day after day.

We were visited by a dear old lady who brought us writing materials and sweets, etc; she is English and wears the Boer War ribbon and seems to have spent her life with soldiers in South Africa, Malta and India.

When we were allowed to get up we were given the familiar baggy blue hospital suits with voluminous white shirts and big red ties in which we felt very conspicuous as we tottered out to explore the shops and lie on the nearby beach.

We watched with envy the lucky ones who were taken out to the hospital ship and wished that our erratic temperature charts would allow us to join them.

August 12

The MO packed off another batch to England. I, too, was sent off with some others but it was to a Convalescent Camp. Sadly we said goodbye to the nurses and the men in the ward and went out to a waiting bus. Just before it left a lady handed in to us a large bag of ripe plums from a nearby fruit shop — a kindly gesture no doubt engendered by the woe-be-gone look on our faces.

August 13–20

Back to sleeping on wooden bedboards between blankets in the hutment camp above Boulogne brought home to us a grim reminder that once again we had been caught up in the war machine. Time passed heavily with four parades a day and a medical inspection at three day intervals with light fatigues.

August 21–27
At the medical inspection I was passed as fit and marched 150 yards down the road to Base Details where we spent the night in tents with one blanket. Next morning parties were detailed for their various bases; mine was Le Havre and after a meal we were marched down to the station and packed into filthy horse trucks in which we spent a miserably uncomfortable night.

At Harfleur we detained and marched up to No. 16 Camp where I met several familiar faces from the Brigade. After two or three days I began to feel very ill again; I couldn't take any food and I reported sick at the MO's room where I found another familiar face in Corporal Child who gave me some medicine. I felt as weak as a kitten and to add to my misery I was told that my name was on a draft for Trench Mortars, known as the Suicide Club.

August 28– September 5
Managed to totter on parade with the other victims for The Suicide Club but at the MO's inspection he refused to listen to me. So I went off to see Corporal Child again and he made me see another doctor who promptly sent me to No. 7 Canadian Hospital where I was put to bed and treated more like a human being. As I lay there I wondered what would happen next morning when I was reported absent from the Trench Mortar draft.

It was here that my mail caught up with me and it was a relief to have a letter from Jim Turner to say that Major Petrie was putting in a claim for my return to the Battery as soon as I was fit again.

September 6–14
I was taken to Z Convalescent Camp above Le Havre where the usual light fatigues and route marches occupied part of each day.

One job was to move a heap of cinders until the route march parade had left the camp when we quietly disappeared. I suspect that the same heap of cinders would be shifted back again to its original position by some later innocent fatigue party.

It was possible to get a pass into Le Havre and one day I was fortunate in getting a ticket to the Grand Theatre where Lena Ashwell's Company were giving a show.

There was a camp library from which books could be borrowed and one could read them sitting about in the grounds or in the YMCA hut but it made a refreshing change to get away into the town with a pass which gave one complete freedom from 2 to 8.30.

Sometimes parties of men are marched down to free cinema shows and these are quite enjoyed but I found it more relaxing to go down on the funicular railway and sit about on the beach watching a couple of silvery airships patrolling the harbour or walk around the shops and have a leisurely cup of tea at the central YMCA.

September 15–23
Back to the Base Camp again with plenty of parades and signalling practice in morse with buzzer and lamp.

One very long day was spent down in Harfleur with a party emptying over forty railway wagons of used ammunition boxes and shell cases which had to be stacked in 20 foot high piles.

September 24–27
Left the Base and entrained at Le Havre in cattle trucks. There were 35 in our truck and after seven hours of sheer misery we were glad to tumble out at Rouen for breakfast.

About 4 p.m. we re-entrained in coaches which were slightly better than cattle trucks, reaching Varennes about 2.30 next morning where our Divisional Ammunition Column was stationed.

It was there that I found Arthur Driver and another signaller who had been in the front line for the last three days and had got separated from the liaison officer; I was able to explain the situation and take them back to the Battery.

(Introductory note to October 1916)
During the months of October and November the weather was cold and depressing with a lot of heavy rain which filled the shell holes and reduced the ground to a sea of slimy mud. Boots and clothes never completely dried out and to this physical discomfort was added a sense of disillusionment over the apparent failure of our operations opposite Thiepval and the heavy losses incurred by the infantry in unrewarding attack after attack.

October 1
The gunners have been firing all night on their SOS lines and we are all feeling somewhat jaded; fortunately we were relieved by another battery who took over our guns and we made our way back to the wagon line which had been moved to a bare hillside near Albert. Jim and I slept under a GS wagon that night.

October 2–8
It rained steadily all day and night as we waited for the order to move which eventually came next morning at about 5 a.m.

The rain was still falling as we splashed our way through the mud feeling wet and cold and thoroughly miserable but very thankful to be going away from the line as an occasional long range shell reminded us that there was still a war on.

On the way through Souastre I stopped at a YMCA hut for something to eat and caught up with the Battery at Bus, our destination.

Spent another rainy night with three others under a tarpaulin but water flowed in from the sides and everybody's clothes and blankets are sodden.

October 20–21
We left Bus without regret and moved up into action in front of Mailly-Maillet. The gun pits and dugouts were already made and lay in a stretch of open country between Colincamps and Auchonvillers

Joe's method for cooking porridge

which were being heavily shelled as we came up.

Four of us linesmen occupied a dugout which appeared to be a section of a roofed-in trench fitted with bunks at one side. Fortunately there was a stove at the end which we managed to get going and were able to partially dry our wet clothes.

Three shells fell on the position without doing any damage and the holes were quickly filled in.

October 22–23
Down to the OP to register targets and were followed closely by shells on our way back up the communication trench.

During the heavy firing programme many of the gunners were overcome by the fumes which collected in the enclosed gun pits and had to be laid on the ground outside to recover.

October 24
During the night a shell dropped just outside the dugout entrance, blowing in the trench and burying all our telephone equipment and drums of wire — after so much rain it was a messy job digging it out.

The mail brought me a welcome parcel containing a pair of gumboots which will be a godsend in this weather.

October 25
The officers have organized a canteen in one of the dugouts and we are living in comparative luxury. We four subscribe to a mess fund and for tea today we had veal and bread and butter, pineapple and custard and cake. With our stove working well we are able to make porridge for supper every night which is a great comfort.

October 31
Wakened at 7.30 a.m. by a tremendous crumping outside and thought that the Huns were shelling us again as they seem to know just where we are but it was only another of our artillery stunts.

Two of us were sent down to the wagon line about 5 or 6 kilometres behind with a message. Just after leaving Mailly-Maillet on our return journey we were shaken by two heavy shells which exploded about 25 yards away; in the darkness they sounded so much nearer than that.

The roof leaks like a sieve

November 1, 2, 3
Slept till dinner time as we didn't get back from the WL until 2 o'clock this morning. While out repairing the HQ line we were disturbed by a sudden burst of 6 or 8 shells falling uncomfortably near and we had to take cover.

The persistent rain is loosening the earth in the dugout walls and the expanded metal revetting sheets are beginning to bulge ominously. The roof leaks like a sieve and we have suspended ground sheets to catch the water but the constant threat of a sudden cold shower as they fill during the night does nothing to raise the general depression.

November 4
Candles are getting very scarce so Jim and I scoured the countryside for fresh supplies. We got as far as Warloy where we had something to eat at the EF Canteen and took the opportunity to visit the cottage where Alice and Naomi used to sell us coffee way back in February.

In our absence the Battery had been heavily shelled with 5.9's and the '*hate*' started again soon after we arrived.

November 7
Wakened at 2.15 a.m. by the guard who told us that gas shells were falling all round the position and warned us to have

Curtains over the entrances help to keep out a lot of the gas

our respirators handy. Dugouts are now fitted with blanket curtains over the entrances which help to keep out a lot of the gas.

Somebody seems to have got our Battery position on their list of targets and daylight revealed a depressing sight of fresh shell craters all round; once again gunpits and dugouts have escaped serious damage but the constant rain is playing havoc with them and some are gradually disintegrating.

November 8

After attending a Communion service in one of the dugouts I pulled out my wire netting bed, strengthened the wall with boards and removed the pile of earth which had fallen in during the night. Water is now pouring into the far end of the dugout behind the stove and conditions are becoming impossible.

November 9

On the left flank of the Battery is a small chalk pit in which are the officers' quarters and the cookhouse. This is being steadily shelled while a *Boche* plane overhead appears to be observing the fire.

Accompanied Mr. Butler to the OP until 4.30 and on our way back we could see that the gun position was obscured by smoke and debris from bursting shells. This was a horrible sight and we waited for the storm to ease off before approaching any nearer, but once again a miracle had happened and no casualties had been incurred.

November 10
Another gas alarm at 2 a.m. but it wasn't bad enough in the dugout to don respirators.

Down to the OP to observe the fire of 200 rounds on the German second line wire entanglements.

Fine day for a change and the *Boche* planes are very active over our lines; they seem to have achieved the ascendency in this sector and fly overhead almost unmolested.

November 12
Parties of infantry are moving up for an attack in the morning and all the tanks which we heard coming up last night are being withdrawn owing to the wet and mud in the battle area.

November 13
Turned out at 4 a.m. to go down to the OP for the attack which started at 5.45. It was too foggy to see much but we had news that Beaumont Hamel and 400 prisoners had been captured.

November 14
Was put on telephone duty in place of Albert Vallender who was out on some new signalling scheme. At 2.30 the infantry attacked again and the guns were firing away all day regardless of eight *Boche* planes which were circling over the Sucrerie just in front.

November 15
Wilf relieved me at the telephone at 3 a.m. and I tumbled into his bed. About 9 o'clock Vallender turned up looking white and shaken; he said that shelling had been incessant at 'The White City' and he had been buried in a dugout which had been blown in.

'The White City' was a conglomeration of dugouts housing battalion HQ and the mountains of white chalk from the excavations provided an obvious target for the German artillery and was subjected to frequent vicious storms of shell fire.

Jim and Eric Cowling are down there now and Wilf and I are to relieve them tomorrow.

November 16, 17
We duly reported at battalion HQ at 'The White City' with rations for 24 hours. Between HQ and the front line three stations A, B and C are to relay messages; B and C are in captured enemy trenches and A in what had been our old front line.

We were allotted to station A which

consisted of a couple of corrugated iron sheets over the top of a badly damaged trench.

Soon after 3 p.m. the *Huns* started shelling and the line between us and station B was broken. Taking it in turns we went out over the open to repair break after break but it all seemed to be so hopeless. It was freezing hard all night and there seemed to be no diminution in the shelling.

The last time Wilf went out on the line he didn't come back and I decided that I had better go and look for him. It was the most eerie experience I have ever had. In faint moonlight I followed the line between the shell craters, some of the more recent ones still smoking and glowing with an uncanny phosphorescent light. I fully expected to find my friend lying wounded or dead but no trace of him could I find.

As the shelling eased off a bit towards morning I was able to get the line working again before being relieved about 8.30.

November 18
Another man came up from the wagon line to replace Wilf who, it appears, had been wounded and gone off to the dressing station.

(Footnote to November 18, 1916)
It was almost two years before I saw Wilf again at Catterick Camp where he was established as Signals Officer and we celebrated Armistice Day with a supper of fish and chips at Richmond.

November 19
At 3 o'clock in the morning Paddy Malone came in from '*The White City*' wounded; he reported that station A had been blown in killing three men and wounding two out of five men and one officer. I got up and took him to the dressing station at the Sucrerie, a wrecked building several hundred yards in front.

While we were having dinner Sugden turned up; he also had been wounded shortly after he had gone to '*The White City*' this morning. This precious scheme has been a very costly one and after the COs of the divisional batteries concerned in it had protested, it was abandoned.

November 20
After we had seen Gunner Sugden leave for the dressing station yesterday it was quite a surprise to see that he had returned to us. Apparently his wound was only a slight one giving no hope of being sent to '*Blighty*' or even to the Base and getting fed up with the place where he was asked to be returned to the Battery and back he came.

November 21
Ten men from Cheshire battery fresh from England came up for instruction and went back in the evening.

The tank 'Admiral Beatty' passed the position and as it was the first one we had seen at close quarters we watched it with great interest as it slowly negotiated the mud and shell holes.

November 22
Some new signallers from the Cheshire battery came up and we showed them round the OP and other lines, explaining the various duties and work involved.

One of our FE planes was brought down in a fight with three German planes but appeared to make a safe landing on our left.

November 23
Jim, Arthur and two other signallers went forward on liaison duty while we started packing up ready to move out of action.

At the last moment I was given a bicycle to take out but after struggling

The 'Admiral Beatty'

with the thing for about 100 yards the wheels became so clogged up with mud that it had to be either carried or slid over the slimy ground. I was physically incapable of doing either for the 5 or 7 kilometres to the WL and in sheer desperation and at the end of my tether I hurled it into a large water-filled shell crater after removing my kit.

(Footnote to November 23)
I was debited with the cost of a bicycle — but it was well worth it. On a later occasion my request to use a cycle was turned down by Mr. Whitaker who, with the suspicion of a twinkle in his eye, remarked in his customary dry manner that the Battery had only three machines on the strength.

November 24, 25
The Battery moved to a muddy field near Pas and by the time we had finished feeding and rugging up the horses it was dark.

The rain was still pouring down as we struggled to erect some bell tents to sleep in. Jim and the others, who had been sent on liaison duty when the Battery came out of action, turned up and I helped them to put up another tent.

November 26
At the last moment I was told to join a party going up to find a new gun position. Guides would be stationed at cross roads to direct me but when I left with a horseholder some time later we travelled as far as Hebuterne without seeing any signs of our people so we returned to Pas. The horses were dead beat after covering 25 to 30 kilometres without a feed.

November 27, 28
The tent canvas was frozen stiff this morning and a move to anywhere from this depressing place will be welcome, even into action again. Into action it is and we are relieving D/232 Battery of the 46th Division and taking over their guns.

The position is in an orchard on the outskirts of Bienvillers where a number of civilians are still living and is regarded as a distinct improvement. The dugouts are all very deep and fitted with beds, hot baths are available in the village and the war appears to be a long way off here.

November 30th
Three of us walked the 4 kilometres to Souastre to see a show by '*The Tykes*', Jim and I having already booked seats yesterday when we had to leave rather hurriedly as a few shells fell in the village. All this is obviously too good to last, as it proved only too well in my case.

December 1
I was attached to a mobile AA battery billetted at Souastre, supposedly for two days but on arriving I was told that it was for a month. Not liking this a bit I obtained permission to return to the Battery for my kit and reported this to Mr. Whitaker who promised to make enquiries. In the meantime I went back to

Souastre where the AA gunners were billetted in a large barn.

December 2–4
For several days foggy weather kept the AA battery in billets and we had lectures on aircraft recognition. At dawn on the third day we were turned out as the weather had cleared and enemy aircraft became active.

The guns are 13 pounders I think, mounted on flat lorries of which the sides can be lowered and supported on legs to provide a platform for the crew. Several roadside sites in the district have been levelled and covered with balks of timber.

December 5
Dull day with no action; at dusk seeing three of our wagons on the way from the WL to the Battery I jumped on one to have tea and spend the evening with my friends. Got a lift back to Souastre in a motor ambulance to learn that a few shells had dropped in the village in my absence.

December 6–23
The short winter days left quite a lot of time to spend in a YMCA hut in the village or wait for the mess cart on its way to the Battery to snatch an hour with 'my ain folk'.

Making friends with another of the attached men called Bowker we went one evening to see '*The Whizz-Bangs*' who had taken the place of our own divisional concert party, '*The Tykes*'.

On the 18th I walked towards Bienvillers to meet Jim and '*Trump*' who were coming in to see the '*Whizz-Bang*' show for which I had already booked seats.

Fine days were spent out on one of the sites pooping off hundreds of rounds without much apparent effect or working on new timber platforms. This was a cold and messy job and I suspect that this was the main reason for having us extra men attached to the unit.

December 24
I was glad to be returned by lorry to my own Battery which was now out of action at Lucheux.

Christmas Day
A church parade for the whole Brigade was followed by a shortened mid-day stables and the Battery then adjourned to an estaminet which had been reserved for our Christmas dinner served by the officers in the traditional manner.

As the beer flowed freely everybody was in a carefree and happy mood, joining heartily in the choruses of songs given by willing or unwilling '*volunteers*'. After a short break at 6.30 to water and feed the horses the festivities continued with speeches and toasts, not forgetting the momentarily hushed one '*To Absent Friends*'.

Jim and I finished the day by going to the first performance of '*The Tykes*' who had just arrived in the village from Souastre.

December 28
It was a fine and frosty morning and the Battery was inspected by General Percival as it left Lucheux. The roads were very slippery and at Humbercourt my horse shied at a threshing machine and fell; I went over its head and as I lay on the ground the next horse trod on one of my knees and I was taken away on a stretcher.

The MO bandaged me up and I was sent back to join several other men who had been left behind at Lucheux.

December 29–31
Fortunately no bones had been broken but I was told to rest the leg and I spent a very dull time for the remaining days of 1916.

Introductory note to 1917

I THINK THAT perhaps the year 1917 was the blackest period of the whole war when morale reached its lowest ebb.

The useless slaughter on the Somme with so little to show for it; the steady drain of trench warfare with no end in sight sapped our spirits of any feelings of enthusiasm and purpose which might be remaining.

There were faint rumours, apparently all too well founded, of mutiny in the French Army. The increasing success of the German U boats in almost bringing

1917: *Useless slaughter on the Somme*

the country to starvation by sinking an ever rising tonnage of our merchant ships brought much suffering and hardship to the people at home, a fact made only too obvious to us when we went on leave and saw the effect on our parents.

January 7
The Battery returned after being in action in front of Arras and is joined by Captain Eddison with a section from a Cheshire unit which makes us a Battery of six guns instead of four which we have always been until now.

January 10
Four old friends left us today to go home to train for commissions, Charlie Dove, Percy King, Reg Rhodes and Alf Richardson.

January 11
Have just heard that among other promotions Ray and I have been given a '*dog's leg*' but I was quite happy without it.

January 13
Left Lucheux with the RX (right section) reaching La Cauchie about mid-day; four signallers and a few gunners then marched up to Berles-au-Bois to take over from the Battery we were relieving.

The rolling country in this part of the front is dotted with tiny villages of which Berles is a typical example. The road threads its way between the houses down into a shallow dip in the ground and up the other side to the crest from which a view over the next valley discloses the distant Adinfer Wood reported to be packed with German batteries.

At the lowest point in the village a narrow sunken lane bears off to the left and dug into the steep eastern bank are four gun pits and a number of dugouts. One of the new Cheshire guns is pushed forward towards the crest and the other about 100 yards to the rear.

January 14
We were shown round the line to various OPs in the trenches which are knee deep in mud. Apparently there are about half a dozen OPs and with these, together with separate lines to the three gun positions, the officers mess and HQ, there is every prospect of a busy time ahead.

Short goat-skin jackets and thigh long gumboots were issued.

Our standard issue

January 17–23
The country is covered with four inches of snow and it is freezing hard. All the telephone lines, laid loosely over the open ground, are now hidden by the frozen snow and the job of tracing breaks is made so much more difficult and uncomfortable.

On the 20th Jim and I were out on the lines from 5.30 until 11.30 p.m. getting more and more exasperated particularly and perhaps rather unfairly, when we found on our return, tired and despondent, our fingers numbed with cold, that everybody was fast asleep and the dugout fire allowed to go out.

January 24
We finished laying a new line to the forward OP by 11.30 only to find that the line to Battalion HQ wasn't working so we started work on that and having run out of wire at 2 o'clock we returned to the Battery for more. After swallowing a hasty dinner we reeled on some wire to our portable drum and set off again, finishing the last break about 8.30 p.m.

This seems to be the general pattern of life here; many of us are suffering from heavy colds, tempers are short and tried to the utmost.

January 26–28
Another day of frustration! Although the new line to the OP was good the Major considered it would be inadvisable to open fire while the infantry were handing over that particular trench. After a short delay we prepared to register the guns on our target only to find that this time it was the telephone that was faulty – and we had to borrow another one. Bad luck still dogged us as we found gaps in the line on our way back and we had to go out later with more wire. There seem to be some unprincipled linesmen in this sector who take lengths from existing lines to repair their own, a dirty trick we have never experienced before.

We had an unexpected and very welcome visit by Teddy Ledger, one of our old Grammar School friends who is in the infantry and billetted in the village.

January 30
Some days ago the Major gave a lecture on discipline to all men with twelve or more months service. It was felt that with the intake of recruits and new men the original enthusiasm of a local unit like ours was being blunted by the apparent lack of success of the allied armies and so morning '*Spit and Polish*' parades are to be instituted.

At today's parade I was severely ticked off for having dirty buttons. I felt particularly hurt over this because I had carefully polished my buttons and badges but in the darkness of the dugout I had failed to notice that a boot brush had been used in mistake and all my brasses were black.

January 31
The *Boche* sent over a few shells which dropped among the houses behind and killed an old French woman.

Out again on one of the lines to an OP

A beautiful moonlight night

in a little copse just over the ridge in front. It was a beautiful moonlight night and the snow covered ground made everything clear to see.

A German machine gun was sweeping the ridge at intervals and several times we had to drop flat rather hurriedly.

We had a pleasant surprise visit in the person of 'Eker' Knowles, yet another old Ilkley Grammar School friend who is in the gas section of the REs billetted nearby.

February 2

About 10 o'clock shells began to drop round the position and 'Sparks', the RFC radio man attached to us, reported that he thought that a hostile plane was ranging a German battery on us.

Our guns were not engaged in any firing programme at the time and as the range of the enemy shooting was getting uncomfortably accurate the OC ordered the personnel to leave the position and take temporary cover a short distance to the right flank.

The shelling continued methodically all day and when at last it eased off we reoccupied what was left of the position. A terrible scene of destruction and desolation met our gaze, made the more dramatic by the sharp contrast between the blackened shell-torn area and the surrounding snow covered landscape.

'A' gun had received a direct hit, the barrel being the only recognisable piece left. The other three gun pits were also hit and the guns damaged while several dugouts were completely demolished.

The shells were found to be 8 inch and 11 inch armour piercing which produced, in some cases, an unusual effect in that having penetrated the frozen surface they blew a huge cavity in the softer ground underneath, the gases escaping through a small opening in the harder earth above.

The men from the three wrecked guns were sent back to the WL while the rest spent the night in a cave nearby.

February 3–12

The three remaining guns were moved to a position near a reserve system of trenches called Pommier Redoubt and camouflaged as haystacks. The gunners and signallers found accommodation in the dugouts of the redoubt which, having been unoccupied for so long, had icicles hanging from the frozen roofs. They were horribly cold and damp until stoves and fire buckets could be organised and then the icicles melted and we lived in a perpetual cold shower.

Things were rather disorganised for a time. The cookhouse remained in the cave near the old position and parties of men were digging to retrieve personal kit and belongings buried in the smashed dugouts.

The area was visited by numbers of staff officers and ordnance experts examining the craters to determine the type of projectiles used. Some of the shell holes were 15 feet deep and the whole operation had been so concentrated and accurate that the gunners were able to leave the cave and stand watching the destruction a mere 250 yards away to one flank.

February 13

Detailed with two other men to report to 230 Brigade HQ at Souastre where we joined similar groups from seven or eight batteries. We were taken round the area and shown where our various battery positions were to be and what telephone lines had to be laid. After being allotted to billets we were free for the rest of the day and went to see a performance by '*The Whizz-Bangs*' concert party.

February 14

An officer took the signallers up to our various positions and set us on laying the necessary telephone lines. I was detailed to help the corporal at La Haie Chateau and no sooner had we got there than the Germans started shelling the place and we had to take cover. Then came the order to reel in all the lines as the scheme had been abandoned; this took us the rest of the day by which time most of the others had been returned to their units and we spent another night in Souastre. What a mess!

February 15

The reluctance of the HQ cook to give us any breakfast may have been due to the

Our H.Q. cook!

fact that we had helped ourselves to his coal during the night to provide a fire in our billet.

Transport arrived for us in the afternoon and we reached the WL at La Cauchie about 5 o'clock.

While I was getting a bite to eat a German plane flew very low over the village and dropped a couple of bombs.

February 16
Back at the Battery again in time to take two of the new officers round the OPs; it started to rain heavily as we splashed our way through miles of support and communication trenches.

February 17
At the OP in Newark Street all day and was visited by General Kaye's ADC who was showing his relieving ADC round the lines. More trouble with lengths of wire being taken out of ours to mend theirs by some unscrupulous signallers.

The new telephonists who have come to join us are a nice lot of fellows and anxious to help us.

February 22
Jim Turner left us to go home for a commission; I shall miss him very much as we have done so much together especially during the last few months of the most frustrating and unrewarding work we have ever been called upon to do; we were even boy scouts together in the far-off days before the war.

In utter dejection I took one of the new men out and we spent the whole day struggling with mud and endless breaks while he, poor chap, did his best to cheer me up.

February 23
When I got up to do another turn at the OP I found that '*Trump*' Whitaker, who was on the last turn of telephone duty, was suffering from the general depression and was so fed up that he had let the stove go out and refused to chop up any more wood and cook our breakfasts as we had agreed to do for the last few days. Making my own meal threw me an hour late at the OP but as it was very foggy it didn't matter very much.

February 24
The right sections and all the signallers except Arthur and myself moved back to Lucheux leaving us to give a helping hand

to the relieving signallers. We disconnected our switchboard and set off to walk the 10 kilometres to Lucheux; fortunately we got a lift in a lorry to within 3 kilometres of our goal.

February 28
Together with the whole 49th Division the Battery left Lucheux on a trek northwards with horses, harness and vehicles looking spick and span and pulled in for the night at Boubers-sur-Canche. Here all the guns of the Division were left under the charge of Sergeant Gaines to be handed over to the 56th (London) Division which we were to relieve somewhere up north.

March 1
We left Boubers about 9 o'clock and after a short halt just outside St. Pol to water and feed the horses we pushed steadily on for 25 to 30 kilometres and spent the night at Bergueneuse.

Here I was ordered to return to Boubers to collect a horse that had been lamed.

March 2
I set off about 6.30 a.m. and reached Boubers soon after 11 but Sergeant Gaines said the horse was not fit to travel so I decided to stay the night and put my mount into a stable.

After a meal I walked into Frevent which was quite a sizeable town compared with the villages we had visited so far. It was very pleasant looking round the shops and after a meal at a cafe I went into a cinema before walking the 3 kilometres back to Boubers.

March 3
Arrangements had been made for Gornall, one of the new signallers, to meet me at Bergueneuse to guide me after the Battery so I got up about 4 a.m. and set off again on the long trek to make contact. After a short stop at St. Pol to feed the horse and snatch a hasty breakfast in a cafe I pressed on and met a rather worried Gornall about 3 kilometres outside Bergueneuse. Together we walked back to his billet and after a meal we parted company, he to catch up the Battery and I to return once again to Boubers for this wretched lame horse.

March 4
The chateau at Boubers is used as a Casualty Clearing Station and I met one of the RAMC sergeants who took me there for dinner and later for tea. This was a welcome change from the iron rations supplied to me at the brewery where I was billeted; later in the day I was told that I was to ration with the RAMC from tomorrow. I was informed that the Battery was at La Gorgue and I was to rejoin them there.

March 5
Had breakfast at the chateau with the 9th Divisional RAMC who couldn't have done more for our comfort and who are being relieved today by the 58th Division.

The lame horse is still unfit to travel

A French brewery cart

and I rode into Frevent to wire the Battery for instructions about it.

By this time I was getting very short of money and tried to raise some from the Town Major without success but managed to get an advance of 5 francs from the RAMC.

March 7
Orders arrived for me to rejoin the Battery and leave the lame horse so I saddled up and left Boubers. After a short halt at St. Pol for a coffee I pushed on to Bergueneuse to retrieve some kit I had left there. I gave the horse a couple of hours rest and myself something to eat and took to the road again about 4 p.m. This time I travelled only about 6 or 8 kilometres as far as Sains-les-Pernes where I put up for the night in a barn with some men of the Middlesex Regiment who were on their way out from Neuve Chapelle.

It was a bitterly cold night and soon after midnight I had to turn out as the horse had got loose and was wondering about the farmyard. I thought it would have had enough walking after covering between 30 and 35 kilometres.

March 8
It was snowing hard as I left Sains-les-Pernes. A few kilometres short of Lillers I was fortunate in meeting a Canadian sergeant who found something to eat for both my horse and myself.

At Lillers I fell into good hands again and was able to leave my mount for a rest with a chap in the ASC while I had a walk round the town and a snack at a YMCA hut — a snack was all I could afford.

As dusk was falling after covering only

about 8 kilometres I found an empty cottage by the roadside where I intended stopping the night but some people from a nearby house insisted on taking me in for a meal. After spending a very interesting evening with these hospitable friends I was provided with a comfortable bed for the night.

March 9
After breakfast they refused any payment from me and I thanked these good folk warmly as I set off on my lonely journey.

Passing through familiar St. Venant I followed the canal to Merville where I left it and struck out for La Gorgue where the Battery was said to be.

I located the WL and was told to proceed up to the gun position. So after a bath and something to eat I went with the mess cart to where the guns were in action near Laventie.

The personnel live in farm buildings and huts and all is so peaceful with civilians still occupying some of the cottages; conditions don't appear to have changed much since we were here in 1915 in a position about twenty minutes walk away. Hedges still line the roads and the fields are reasonably covered with long grass.

March 12
Spent the day at the OP with Captain Eddison and Corporal John Hornby, another old school friend. This OP is a square three storey concrete tower built inside a half wrecked house about 500 yards behind the front line. An iron ladder leads to the top floor in which a narrow slit provides an extensive view of the country in front.

Several of the guns were registered on their zero lines and we spotted the smoke of a train near Fromelles on which we fired a few rounds without being able to see the result owing to a heavy shower obscuring the view at the critical moment.

March 13
We now have a corporal in charge of signalling whose time seems to be mainly occupied in working out duty rosters and systems. After working together in complete harmony for nearly two years we old hands tend to take a poor view of such officious methods from a complete stranger and the man is not very popular.

March 14
My day off duty so I went round visiting the subsections; later I joined up with Ray and Percy Swift who were going into Laventie for supper. It was a pitch black night and we had the greatest difficulty in finding our way back, sober as we were.

Having finally decided to apply for a commission myself I obtained the necessary papers and sent them off tonight.

March 15
In this quiet sector the subsections take it in turns to be on call. I was on telephone duty with 'F' gun which fired about twenty rounds registering several targets.

Later I went into Laventie with Arthur Driver and Percy Dalton and found that a girl called Madeline, who used to make us coffee in her cottage near the gun position at Fleurbaix in 1915, is now working in an estaminet here.

March 16–23

This comparatively peaceful country with its network of lanes intersecting the flat rectangular fields mostly surrounded by hedges is a pleasant change from the blasted downland of the Somme area and there seems to be a policy of *'live and let live'* observed by the two sides. What shelling takes place from time to time has an almost apologetic air about it, perhaps to serve as a reminder that there is a war on and to keep the opposing gunners in practice.

Occasionally we borrow the Battery bikes and cycle down to the OP on our line patrol since the telephone line follows a road most of the way. One stretch of the road is open to enemy observation and we pedal furiously over this though I'm sure that *Jerry* is unlikely to waste ammunition on a couple of cyclists.

March 24

My turn for OP with Mr. Whitaker but as he wasn't ready he gave me the binoculars and told me to go ahead and have a look round. Apart from smoke from dugout fires and a number of *Huns* moving casually about there was nothing much to be seen.

When Mr. Whitaker arrived he pointed out a number of targets in our sector and it passed the morning very well. Later in the day we appeared to be a target too as a number of 4.2's fell in the vicinity and we retired to the basement.

The OP is in one of the first houses in Fauquissart and from the door through which we enter we can see beyond piles of rubble several other damaged buildings of which I made a pencil sketch to pass the time.

March 30

Mr. Holmes took me to join some others at the WL as an advance party to another sector of the line. Keeping up a smart pace we reached Bethune about 11 o'clock

Targets in Fauquissart

where we had a look round while the horses rested and then pressed on to establish a WL on a bare open hillside near Gouy-Servins. The village was packed with Canadians, every possible billet being full and we had to make do with bell tents.

March 31
I went with Mr. Homes to find a position for the guns. Following a long winding valley towards Lens, held by the Germans, we passed numerous 12, 9.2, 8 and 6 inch howitzers, besides many field batteries, so everything seems to indicate another offensive in preparation. Our road led through the village of Carency of which practically nothing remains, just a wilderness of shell holes and rubble heaps. The position lies a little way beyond Carency and is only just screened from the Germans holding Vimy Ridge by a shallow fold in the ground.

We returned to the WL to find that 18 bell tents had been provided to accommodate the Battery on this bare hillside which is now being swept by driving sleet and rain.

April 1
After dinner I went in search of timber for harness racks, at least that was my avowed intention. It was, of course, a mere coincidence that I found a YMCA hut about a mile away and had something to eat.

Later in the day, being the only one who knew the way, I was sent to guide a wagon load of stores to the gun position, a round trip of more than 10 kilometres, and we got back to the WL about 11 p.m. very wet, very hungry and very fed up.

April 2
On the way up to the position with the right and centre sections we were held up on the road for about an hour by a maze of telegraph wires brought down in the blizzard which has been raging most of the day.

Accommodation is very short but I managed to get a place in an old French dugout which had been excavated in the chalk of a low bank. It was bitterly cold and our clothes were wet through from the driving snow but we were thankful to flop down anywhere out of the wind.

April 3
After Mr. Whitaker had shown us where the OP was we got the line laid ready for registering the guns. With three inches of snow on the ground it was a cold job – cold too for the left section which came up after dark.

April 4
There are 4 or 5 other howitzer batteries near us in the low ground in front of Carency and we connected up by telephone to the nearest one.

From our No. 4 gun we can see some of the houses in Lens.

April 5
This morning I helped to work No. 2 gun with Ray and Sergeant Gee as they were rather short handed, then we had to lay another line to Corps Heavy Artillery.

April 6
As a '*Posh Parade*' had been ordered for this morning – this really was the limit – Arthur and I thought it might be a good idea to go and check the OP line.

Today is Good Friday and the news reaches us that America had declared war on Germany. This didn't seem to make as much impression on the Battery as a 20 minute bombardment of the German trenches by our artillery. All those not engaged in working the guns mounted the slope in front to get a good view of Vimy Ridge in the distance being inundated by a storm of shells from 12 inch to 18 pounders. This was much more to our liking.

April 8
Clocks were put on one hour this morning.

Registering by the guns continued from an observation balloon in spite of many German planes flying around in front. We quite expected to be shelled in retaliation but the job had to go on to be ready for an assault on the Ridge in the morning.

April 9 – Easter Monday
At 5.30 a.m. the fun started – in more ways than one. I had just crawled out of my blankets to light a candle when there was a rush of falling earth and stones and on looking round I saw a pile of chalk where I had been lying. After rescuing my clothes I dressed and went outside to watch the bombardment from the top of the bank. It was just light enough to see the summit of Vimy Ridge which was one mass of smoke and flame from bursting shells of all calibres.

News began to trickle through of ground gained and prisoners captured and the absence of hostile fire seemed to confirm this.

One of our observation balloons broke loose but the crew made successful parachute landings before being blown over the German lines.

April 10
Further news confirmed that the attack had been a complete success with 7200 prisoners and the summit of Vimy Ridge in our hands. Several 4.2 shells fell near the Battery wounding Mr. Butler and Mr. Whitaker. Mr. Butler was able to walk to the dressing station but Mr. Whitaker had been hit in both legs and we had to take him on a stretcher. This was a sad loss as both officers were very popular, the latter having been with us from the beginning.

April 11
Went up with Arthur and the Major to the Ridge to try and locate a new trench the Germans are reported to be digging. We passed the captured German front line and moved forward a long way to the other side of the summit but we could see no signs of activity anywhere. The ground was littered with Canadian and German dead and many of the enemy's deep dugouts had been blown in and their trenches smashed out of all recognition. There was also quite a lot of French

equipment lying about from the time when they held the Ridge.

April 12
The whole area is covered in six inches of snow this morning. Arthur and myself were warned to go up to the Ridge again but later it was decided that one was enough and I accompanied the observing officer.

About half way between the Battery and the Ridge we entered an underground tunnel which brought us out into the old '*No Man's Land*'. It was a marvellous place nearly a mile long containing dressing stations and rooms fitted with bunks sufficient to hold hundreds of men. Water and electric light were laid on and the whole system was known as *Tottenham Tunnel*.

Emerging from the tunnel we made our way over nearly 1000 yards of shell holes and smashed in trenches to the far side of the Ridge from which a splendid panorama of the country beyond was laid before us. I had never seen so many square miles of *Hun* country before – he usually makes sure of that.

A few shells began to fall around and with several others I moved into a nearby German dugout, finding a place half way down the steep staircase. As I sat there I was suddenly conscious of an arm being stretched forward over my head and bringing out from a recess in the timbered roof a magnificent black and gold pickelhaube. What a splendid souvenir I had just missed!

We returned to the Battery by way of a second tunnel called '*Cavalier Tube*' running parallel to the one we had come up through.

April 13
The enemy are reported to be falling back as our patrols push forward. Heavy explosions and fires seem to indicate that *Jerry* is destroying dumps of ammunition and stores as he retires beyond the range of our guns.

Corporal Webster has announced that 4 or 5 mounted signallers would be going forward in the morning and the WL will be brought up during the night to take the guns forward.

April 14
The advance party of officers and signallers rode forward through the ruins of Souchez to a shallow depression in the ground below the northern end of Vimy Ridge where we dismounted while the battery OC went ahead on foot to establish positions for their guns.

In this scene of desolation the smashed remains of the German front line is marked by the distorted and half buried figures of the dead defenders; no longer do they bear any resemblance to living human beings but rather like dolls that have been pulled apart and hurled to the ground by some frenzied insensate giant in a fit of spiteful rage. '*No Man's Land*' is littered with the Canadian dead which have not yet been collected and buried. Here too were numerous signs of French occupation before they lost the Ridge to the Germans.

It was a relief to leave this haunted and horrible place and, as we moved back again, we passed large working parties of gunners levelling a road over the shell-cratered ground for the guns to advance and now we had to reel in any wire which was out of use as there seems to be a shortage.

By tea time the area round the Battery position was seething with activity as WLs heavy guns, dumps and captive balloons pressed forward or took up positions for further action.

April 15–17

While the Battery was preparing to move forward orders came to rejoin our own Division where we left it in the Fleurbaix sector. Unfortunately so many of our horses had died from exposure on the bleak open hillside near Gouy-Servins that we had to borrow horses and even mules from the DAC.

As we waited miserably in the bitter driving rain for fresh draught animals and losing still more as we waited, the gloomy thought came to us that this was the second anniversary of our leaving England for a war that some considered would be over by the following Christmas. What a grim joke! We are not amused!

April 18

Still raining hard as we struck camp and hauled the vehicles out of the deep mud onto the road; two wagons got bogged down but we managed to drag them out in time for the Battery to move off at 8 a.m. The outriders' horses were needed for the teams and all except the team drivers had to tramp it through the slush. We pushed on at a good pace for about 20 kilometres pulling in at Bethune to water and feed. Several more horses died of exhaustion on the way and now the drivers too had to dismount and lead their teams.

The Battery staggered into the old billets at La Gorgue footsore and weary having travelled a distance of 38 kilometres during the day.

April 19

It was quite a struggle to get up this morning and at 10 o'clock the signallers paraded and marched up to the gun position. Did I say 'marched'? We hobbled up like old men and then we hobbled round the OP line and put it into working order. In the evening four of the guns came up and we helped to manhandle them into their gunpits; the others were sent off to Ordnance to be calibrated.

Several of the signallers visited Marie's cottage nearby; she made the best coffee we had ever tasted but perhaps it was the contrast between the relative peace and comfort of her cottage and the hell we had just left which made it so good.

April 20

Maybe this isn't the peaceful haven we thought it was. On checking the remaining lines this morning Arthur and I found them chewed up rather badly by shells; it

Portuguese Infantry

Portuguese transport

seems that *Jerry* has been quite active in our absence.

April 26
On the way back from checking the OP line with Corporal Webster we could see shells falling on what we thought was the Battery position; on approaching nearer, however, we realised that it was a section of 18 pounders which was receiving attention. They occupy a position in or near Red House, a building on the roadside about 400 yards on our right. A steady stream of 5.9s fell in the area but we heard later that apart from slight damage to one of the guns the effect was negligible.

April 27
On my way round the lines this morning I met a number of Portuguese infantry going into the trenches. They wore blue grey uniform with khaki webbing equipment and large yellow soft leather boots. They became known as '*The Pork and Beans*' until this epithet was forbidden.

April 29
I was detailed to report to Divisional Signals at La Gorgue for a course on the Fullerphone which was to be held at Le Sart near Merville to where we were taken by lorry.

One usually finds a kindred spirit on these occasions as I did here and together we made our way into Merville, about 20 minutes walk away, for a meal and to shop and, strangely, to a photographers to have our photos taken.

April 30 – May 6
Near the farm where the course is being held is a wood and now that the weather is turning warmer and the trees and hedges quickly throwing out their leaves, my friend and I like to find a sunny spot amongst the trees and settle down with a book after the days parades are over. Once two or three deer came to have a look at us and we heard the cuckoo for the first time.

'The Tykes' are now in business

May 7
Back at the gun position again after a very pleasant break.

About 7.45 p.m. all the gas gongs on our left started sounding their warning. Several wagons were up at the time unloading ammunition and we had to get them away quickly but fortunately the gas didn't come our way.

May 9–16
A little way in front of the Battery is a rectangular moat surrounding what was probably an old defended farm of which nothing now remains. This is quite a common feature in this part of the country and provides a useful swimming pool. Now that the weather has turned quite warm we slide off for a swim at every opportunity.

The Divisional concert party '*The Tykes*' are now in business at Laventie and we have made several visits to see them.

A scheme has been devised for bringing up 12 horses at a time from the WL to graze in one of the deserted fields near the guns; it seems a pity to let all this fresh grass go to waste.

Some of my evenings are passed very pleasantly playing chess with Arthur Shaw who has a pocket set. All in all the war is quite tolerable in this sector.

May 17
Strolling round the lanes this evening, as

we sometimes do, I met Eric Wilkinson,* now a Captain in the West Yorkshire Regiment. When I was a mere fourth former at Ilkley Grammar School he was a prefect and school captain and very prominent in sports, school plays and other activities. His father was a keen cyclist and wrote articles and books on the subject under the pen name of 'Kuklos'. In Norfolk jacket and knickerbockers his weather-beaten baldish head bent low over the handlebars was a familiar sight in Ben Rhydding where the family lived.

May 20

No. 5 gun has been moved into the open under camouflage netting to fire 50 rounds a day into two German trenches called *Bertha* and *Irma*. During the actual firing I was given the job of airscout to give warning of enemy planes. A slight diversion was created when the camouflage netting caught fire and there was a scramble to put it out before it reached the pile of shells and charges.

May 24

My leave pass came through and I travelled home with Harry Butterfield. Unbelievably I spent my 21st birthday returning to France on June 5th. I must be daft!

June 10

The left section was to be detached temporarily for a strafe so Arthur and I together with 5 gunners were to go with Captain Eddison to prepare a position at Richebourg St. Vaast which is near where we were in action two years ago. Our sister battery, the 10th, now designated D/246 (we are now known as D/245) were already in action there and as we had to lay a line to them we renewed acquaintance with some of the signallers.

June 12–13

I accompanied Lieutenant Spencer to the OP using much the same route as we did in 1915. We had to make a detour round the house by the barricade where I saw my first German prisoner two years ago as *Jerry* was dropping 5.9s on it, one coming uncomfortably close to us.

In Richebourg l'Avoue the factory had been crumped pretty flat and the cottages, from which we used to observe and into which I had been unceremoniously blown by a shell on May 9th 1915, reduced to rubble. The estaminet across the street from which we had tried to signal back to the Battery by means of a torch through a drainpipe was still standing and now had a square concrete tower built inside it and this was our O.P.

About 7.30 p.m. the *Boche* started a terrific bombardment of our front line and captured nearly 800 yards of trench which was occupied, or rather lost, by the Portuguese. After holding this for three hours the enemy evacuated it again and things gradually quietened down until 1.15 a.m. when we made a successful counter raid. Gunfire was more or less continuous until 3.15 when our main raid went in. To conserve the ammunition we had brought, our two guns hadn't joined

---

*Eric won the Military Cross in 1915 near Ypres at the time when we were in action at Briden.
Wounded at Thiepval on the Somme in 1916 he was killed at Passchendale on October 9, 1917.
A book of his poems called 'Sunrise Dreams' was published.

in the early actions but now they kept up a barrage until 4.30 when the raid was over and everybody turned in and slept.

The guns were taken out soon after dusk and after seeing our stores and kit into a G.S. wagon, Arthur and I walked back to the main position near Laventie.

Later this evening 15 wagon loads of shells came up and it was well after midnight before we had finished packing them away in the gunpits and dumps.

June 14
The right section has been moved about a mile away on the other side of Laventie and Arthur and I were sent over to man the telephone in a comfortable little whitewashed outhouse in the yard of one of the last buildings in the village.

June 15
We were not going to be done out of our daily swim in the moat up at the Battery position, this is our greatest pleasure here, so after breakfast I borrowed a bike and cycled up for my dip. In the afternoon I took over the phone while Arthur went for his swim.

June 16
It was a pleasure to be told to collect a map from the main position since it gave me a legitimate reason for having my morning swim. On the way back through the village I bought some strawberries which we had for dinner. Then it was Arthur's turn to go for his dip and, of course, he arrived back with more strawberries for tea. *It's a good life!*

More targets were registered by Captain Eddison from a balloon this evening; the map I collected from the Battery position this morning must have been intended for this purpose.

June 17
More swims and more strawberries but this time the cycle was in use and we had to walk.

No. 1 gun being on call, the two of us had to be on the telephone all night. Arthur seemed to have had a lot of trouble with black beetles down his shirt during his turn of duty.

June 19
After last night's turn of duty on the 'phone I slept like a log until Arthur wakened me at 9 o'clock with my breakfast and then I slept again till he roused me out with my dinner.

Another swim, more strawberries and as the guns were firing again, more telephone duty until 2 a.m.

June 20
The weather has turned much cooler with rain and a thunderstorm. More targets were registered from a balloon until it had to be hauled down at the approach of another storm. A *Boche* plane bombed two of our balloons and brought them down in flames.

June 23
The tedium of my night duty was relieved by a little excitement for a change. At 11 p.m. No. 1 gun fired fifty

gas shells on a German battery which had been making a nuisance of itself during the day and the camouflage netting caught fire. It was soon extinguished but in the darkness the flames seemed so much bigger and brighter.

Some of the spare daytime hours were spent with the gunners playing cricket using a broken spade for a bat and a ball made of rubber charge caps wrapped tightly round a No. 5 charge and tied together with string.

June 26–27
The section pulled out and as it passed the rest of the Battery on the other side of Laventie it picked up some ammunition wagons and made its way several kilometres further north to a new temporary position not far from where we were in June 1915.

Next day I went with Captain Eddison to register the guns using the convent in Bois Grenier as OP which hasn't changed much since we used it in 1915.

About 10 p.m. the rest of the Battery came up followed at 2 a.m. by more wagon loads of shells.

June 29
Spent the morning helping the gunners to carry ammunition to the gun pits in the rope handled boxes each containing two shells and their propellant charges. The *Boche* were dropping 5.9s onto a 6 inch howitzer battery about 400 yards on our right and spent fragments kept whistling down all the time.

The raid which we had come to support lasted from 3.05 to 4.10 p.m. and then we started packing up again.

In the evening I took a stroll up to the position we occupied in 1915; all the gun pits were overgrown with grass and part of the thatched roof was all that remained of the cottage in the corner of the orchard where Madeline and her parents used to live, the same Madeline whom we recently discovered working in an estaminet in Laventie.

June 30
Having reeled in all the lines there was nothing else to do until dark so I joined several others for a walk round Fleurbaix which is not far away.

During the evening a couple of G.S. wagons came up for stores and I was given a map and told to take them to another position a few kilometres away which we reached about 10 o'clock.

The guns followed soon after midnight, were allotted their places and the men billeted in one of the buildings which loomed mysteriously out of the darkness.

July 1
The guns were in a large enclosed garden filled with apple trees and soft fruit bushes. The cluster of houses outside seem to be on the southern outskirts of Armentières.

Four of us laid claim to a small shed in one corner while the rest of the signallers took over the enclosed space under an ornamental open summerhouse rather like a small bandstand.

At intervals all day the *Boche* dropped shells in the town but in spite of this a number of civilians still clung to their shops and houses. Arthur and I went for a look round and had some coffee and eggs but the place feels haunted and empty.

July 2
It seems to be standard practice to erect these three storey concrete towers inside wrecked houses for use as OP's and most of the day was spent in one with the telephone.

I was just getting my bed down for the night when I received orders to take a bike and go out to meet some ammunition wagons from the DAC and guide them in.

July 3
Went for another exploratory walk into Armentières. Practically all the shops were closely shuttered but a few were open and one or two canteens and YMCAs were installed in some of the larger buildings.

Just outside the orchard in which the guns are situated ran a tiny stream, said to be the humble beginning of the River Lys, but I doubt it. We dammed it with sandbags to form a pool about one foot deep which served to give us a bath.

July 6
I volunteered to cycle over to the old position near Laventie to get some money from Arthur Shaw, the Battery clerk, to pay the men here. While this was being got ready I had a swim in the pond and reached Armentières in time for a pay parade at 4.15.

There isn't much to do while we wait to support the raid for which we came and most of the men repaired to an estaminet to spend the money they have just drawn.

At 10 p.m. the Germans attacked the trenches in front from which our troops had been withdrawn beforehand and all the guns in this sector poured in a heavy

The ruins of Armentières Cathedral

Somewhere to store our shells

fire on the evacuated trench.

Things quietened down soon after midnight but a lot of gas shells were coming over and some of the detachments had to work the guns in respirators.

July 7–8
Paid another visit to Armentières to get some tinned fruit and evaporated milk from the YMCA. A few shells were falling amongst the houses so I didn't stay longer than necessary.

During the night a torrential downpour and thunderstorm flooded us out of our garden shed and soaked our blankets. This also helped to bring down part of one of the damaged buildings and bury some of the shells stored there.

The raid is due to take place tonight and, later, we heard that it was a complete success at a cost of one casualty.

July 9
All the lines were reeled in and telephones disconnected and packed up ready for leaving. I had a final bath in our tiny stream and when the Battery moved out at 10 p.m. I followed 'D' gun which contrived to get separated from the others in the darkness. In spite of that, we reached the W.L. about 2 a.m. a few minutes before the rest of the Battery arrived.

The guns had fired off most of the shells that were left as that was the easiest and most useful way to get rid of them; the limbers would have been full already when they came up for the guns.

July 10
Everything had to be cleaned and polished for the move tomorrow. That done, Arthur Shaw and I repaired to the YMCA in La Gorgue for a game of chess and a '*tea and wad*' and booked seats for the evening performance of '*The Tykes*'.

July 11
Leaving La Gorgue we moved into billets about 3 kilometres outside Merville. There was a canal nearby and after mid-

day stables I made a beeline for it. This apparent obsession for water is perfectly understandable when one never quite knows when the next opportunity for a bath will be, especially in summer when the thick khaki uniforms and flannel shirts make a complete immersion in water doubly welcome and refreshing.

I went in again after tea with many others.

July 12–16
Endless '*Stables*', harness cleaning and '*Spit and Polish*' parades. Had a chat in

An evening performance

the estaminet with Micky Smith; he is another of my friends from Ilkley Grammar School days and he is leaving us for a commission. He's a grand chap and very popular.

I well remember the first time I ever spent a holiday away from my family when I went with Micky for a week at Scarborough. I suppose we would be about 12 or 13 and still at school and how we enjoyed being on our own.

Another trip into Merville to get a haircut but with no success; we had more luck with a meal of eggs and chips.

July 17
The whole Division seems to be on the move. Our Brigade now made for Cassell which we could see on the top of a small hill in the distance. It was a long hard climb up into the town but looking back we had a splendid view of the surrounding flat country; we could even see our observation balloons and smoke from bursting shells in the firing line.

Cassell itself is a funny little old world town full of narrow cobbled streets and archways looking like an illustration from a book of fairy tales.

Passing down the hill on the far side we found ourselves on a long straight road bordered by tall trees which stretched as far as the eye could see. At the other end of this road lay the town of Wormhoudt near which we pulled in to water and feed the horses and have a meal.

July 18
It was pitch dark as we moved out to an assembly point soon after midnight to continue our trek northwards; as we entered Wormhoudt there was a halt and the column was held up for a long weary wait in the rain, ignorant of the tragedy that was taking place a little way ahead.

It transpired that one of the trains which run through the streets of many Belgian towns had crashed into a gun team of 'C' Battery which was just in front of us, killing two horses and injuring the three drivers, a sergeant and a gunner and smashing the gun and limber.

It took some time to clear away the mess before we could resume our journey and we were all so weary that some of us had to dismount and walk to avoid falling asleep in the saddle and crashing to the ground.

The column was inspected by the GOC Division just before we reached our destination, Ghyveldt, which was so packed with troops that we had great difficulty in finding anywhere to sleep.

In any case there was little time for that since soon after 11 o'clock, I was in a lorry with OCs of a number of batteries going up to take over from the batteries we were relieving.

I was shown the way to the OP which was in a tall house in Nieuport in a street leading down to the water front.

July 19
I spent the night with this unit in the barn attached to a building on the roadside next to the Furnes canal.

All day long *Fritz* was shelling a howitzer battery just in front of us, knocking out three guns and blowing up a pile of ammunition. The officers and men came into our billet for the night until they could fix up another position.

July 20

From the site our guns are to occupy one looks forward over a flat plain about half a mile wide between the canal on the right and the outskirts of Nieuport on the left. This severely restricted area is packed with field gun batteries served from the rear by a road following the south bank of the canal to a point opposite the building where we are billetted when it crosses over to the north side by Pelican Bridge and continues to follow the canal on our right.

Just past our billet a road forks left cutting diagonally across the open plain into the town which, apart from the tops of one or two of the nearest buildings and the gasometer, is out of sight as it slopes away down to the Yser canal and the distant coast line.

This main approach road is crammed with traffic every night and Pelican Bridge is an obvious target of first importance to the German artillery, making our billet a most unhealthy place.

Guns, ammunition wagons, motor ambulances and transport of all kinds travelling in both directions on this narrow road constitute a problem which is further complicated by the arrival of ammunition barges to unload just short of the bridge.

The right section came up and two of the relieved guns pulled out. The billet was terribly crowded and most of the gunners elected to sleep in the gun pits.

July 21

For some reason no cooks came up with the right section last night so Donny (Donbavand) and I got up and cooked the breakfast.

Registering the two guns was kept to the minimum as German planes were very active all day and seemed to have gained command of the air at this period. They are obviously directing the accurate shelling which has destroyed a number of our guns and ammunition dumps.

We had a surprise visit from Frank Keighley who left us with a wound in the neck last July on the Somme. His battery is in action about half a mile in front of us and has lost five guns in the shelling today.

Soon after dark the rest of the Battery came up and when the teams had got safely away with the limbers we were unloading shells from a barge until 2.30 a.m. The night traffic on the road was being persistently shelled, several teams being blown into the canal and the barge in danger of being sunk.

July 22

The OP in Nieuport has been abandoned as it is impossible to keep the telephone line in working order. We now observe from a house called Blanc Maison on the other side of the canal standing on the edge of the inundated area caused when King Albert ordered the flood gates to be opened to flood the country between Nieuport and Dixmude to arrest the German advance in 1914.

July 23
Another OP called Hardy is in the front line and is named after Colonel Hardy who is buried behind the trench. The canal opposite the billet contains a lot of debris including several dead horses floating about but in spite of this Geoff Watkinson and I decided to have a swim until Fritz started shelling the bridge again and we had to make a hurried and undignified exit.

More barges of ammunition came up after dark and we were unloading these until 4 a.m.

July 24
A very unsatisfactory day of repeated breaks in the OP line which has to follow the road alongside the canal and is too close to all the batteries which are being persistently strafed.

About half a mile from Pelican Bridge the wire crosses the canal over a lock gate and down over the open country skirting the flooded area to Blanc Maison OP.

July 26–27
We laid a fresh line to Hardy OP but it was far from satisfactory and for two days we tried to remedy the fault without much success.

The unfortunate D72 battery was shelled out for the second time this week and in the evening *Fritz* started shelling Group HQ which occupies a farm on the other side of Pelican Bridge.

As our billet is only the width of the canal away some of the shells fell uncomfortably close and we cleared out for a while.

July 28
At the OP all morning but relieved at mid-day and as there seemed to be a lull in the shelling I snatched a quick dip.

About 11 p.m. the guns opened up in support of a raid which didn't last very long and we were able to get to sleep again – but not for long. Gas shells began to fall round the billet and we had to don respirators for a couple of hours.

July 29
It rained steadily all day while we were on the OP line but we managed to keep it working long enough to complete a programme of registering targets by 7 p.m. when the light failed.

Two 18 pounder batteries in front of us were shelled out with a number of casualties. Several shells fell on our position, one falling short on the telephone dugout of our sister battery, D/246, killing 2 and wounding 7 of the signallers. Colin Clark, whom we knew well, was untouched but suffered from shell shock.

August 1–2
Wakened at 3 a.m. by the sound of every gun in the area opening out for 15

minutes – another raid I suppose. Found myself lying in a pool of water; most of the tiles from the barn roof had been shaken off and the heavy rain coming straight through, had soaked everybody's bedding and formed pools on the earthen floor. The rain continued all day filling the ditches which line the roads and flooding out the gunners from their low corrugated iron shelters. There is no chance of drying our clothes and blankets and another miserable wet night is in prospect.

A second day has dragged interminably past and at night the barn was filled with infantry who came in out of the rain. Their billets are in Nieuport but they have to be evacuated every night on account of the gas which hangs about in the cellars.

August 3
Still pouring down and mending a line in the rain couldn't make us much wetter. Conditions for cooking in the open were terribly disheartening and we didn't get any breakfast until 11.

Fritz kept sending over bursts of 6 or 8 shells at intervals during the night on the road outside, killing more men and horses.

These sudden storms descend without any warning and the suspense of wondering when the next one will arrive is most demoralising.

August 4
The war has now been going on for three years without the slightest sign of an end in sight. Its a depressing thought in a depressing situation.

Arrived at Blanc Maison OP with Captain Duncan, who is acting OC and Lieutenant Holmes to find that, of course, the line was dead. Two hours later Donny joined me having followed it all the way down from the Battery without finding a single break.

To make matters worse the telephone refused to work so Mr. Holmes went back and sent someone down with another instrument. By the time we had managed to make some sort of contact it was getting too late to do anything useful and we all returned thoroughly frustrated and disgusted. This is the sort of thing which is shortening our lives by years.

After being out on another broken line until midnight I got down for a rest only to be disturbed by more shelling.

August 5
Made an early start to check the Hardy OP line for Captain Duncan who was going to observe after breakfast. It was cut to bits but by 9.30 we had got it working and returned to the Battery. However, by the time the OP party had reached Hardy the line was broken again and we were out on it till 3 o'clock. Further breaks were repaired by 7.30 and a certain amount of shooting was then possible – but this is all so hopeless!

During the afternoon *Fritz* shelled Pelican Bridge, Group HQ and blew up a dump of 4.5 inch shells.

August 7
A night of alarms and excursions followed a heart-breaking day on those pestilential lines. Shells were dropping all round the billet and five times we got up with the idea of moving away – but where to? Once we ran up towards the Battery but pip-squeaks seemed to be scattered over a wide area and we returned to sit it out in the barn.

About 4 a.m. '*Trump*' came in; he sleeps just across the Bridge at Group H.Q. and that seems to be the main target for the shelling. His billet had been blown in, 'C' battery had an ammunition wagon destroyed and there were many casualties. Things quietened down a bit towards 5 a.m. and we were able to get a little sleep.

August 8
Daylight revealed an awful mess round Group HQ the pave road was torn up and strewn with shattered vehicles and wreckage of all sorts; motor cars and wagons lay deserted in the ditch and dead horses lay about in the road.

It speaks well for the accuracy of German gunnery that we, a mere canal width away, should have escaped a direct hit on the barn.

August 9
On our way back from laying a fresh line to Blanc Maison we could see shells bursting round Pelican Bridge. The cookhouse was behind the house on our side of the bridge and as it was getting on for mid-day and we'd had no breakfast we went in to try and find something to eat and drink until one shell just missed the house, so we left. Then *Fritz* turned his attention to our building and very soon the barn was set alight.

We had to go out on the line again then until about 7 p.m. when we managed to get something to eat and then went over to our wrecked billet to see what we could salvage. It was still smouldering and most of our kit had gone up in flames and we had to rig up some sort of shelter in the open for the night.

August 10
Borrowing a cycle I rode down to the WL to get some new kit from the QM. I went by way of a narrow road running parallel to the canal through Oost Dunkerque on both sides of which were many heavy guns and howitzers in position.

Coming back by the other road I passed several French naval monitors which had sailed up the canal to fire their 100 mm guns.

Shortly after 11 p.m. the SOS rocket went up in front and in seconds every gun was flashing all over the countryside. Shells began to fall in front of the billet and Kenny was wounded in the face. Half an hour after it began all was quiet again and we were able to get some sleep.

August 12
This morning five shells fell round the guns, two pluses, two minuses and one OK so we thought that Fritz must have registered the position ready for annihilation at his leisure but then he lifted

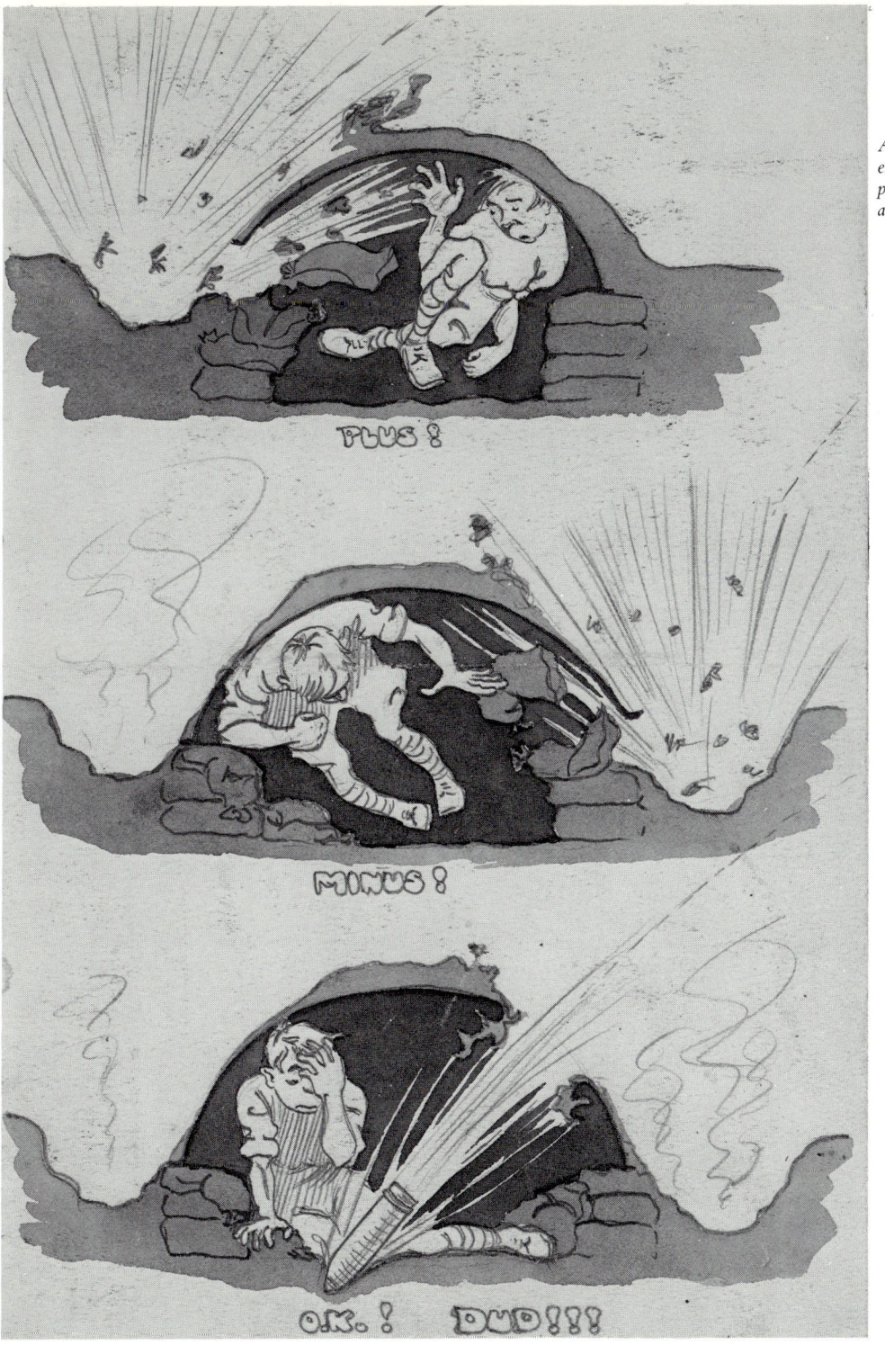

Artillery terms explained: 'two plusses, two minuses and one O.K.'

onto another battery behind us and he shelled it all day setting fire to a pile of boxed ammunition which crackled and exploded for the rest of the day.

After dark we moved four guns to another position further to the right. The flat plain we are on has become a most unhealthy place and so pitted with shell craters that it looks more like '*No Man's Land*'. Battery after battery has been clodded out and any number of guns and ammunition dumps destroyed and we just have to sit tight wondering when our turn will come.

August 13, 14
Apart from the ominous note under the date in my diary which says '*Grouse shooting begins*' I feel that 13 really is unlucky for me today. After a thoroughly unsatisfactory morning on the OP line I was trying to fix one of the other lines up on a pole to cross a ditch when I fell back off the pole into the scummy water and got soaked to the skin. These stagnant ditches are fringed with tall reeds and smell like river estuaries.

Feeling thoroughly disgusted and desperate I went forward with Arthur to where the flood waters were comparatively clean for a swim until my clothes dried out and sweetened a bit.

Soon after the nightly '*strafing*' of the road started we retired to a little curved corrugated iron shelter which we had constructed on the bank of another ditch behind the guns. This is rather like a low dog kennel just big enough for two and no sooner had we crept into this than shells began to drop in the vicinity.

We stuck it out for twenty minutes but when another storm of shells fell much closer we hurriedly dressed and cleared out.

Then the HQ line went and realising that we were not going to get much rest we volunteered to got out on it. This was an unfamiliar line to us and as we stumbled about in the dark we fell into more ditches and got wet through again.

We had just reached the secondary road at the back when suddenly another storm of shells burst upon us and I really thought that this must be the end. I tried to get away but the explosions seemed to follow each other so quickly that I just had to lie flat and hope for the best. As the storm passed I found Arthur and we could hardly believe that, apart from being half buried in mud thrown up by the bursting shells, we had escaped unhurt. I thought then that perhaps 13 wasn't quite such an unlucky number for me after all.

August 15
Early this morning the guard discovered the body of Gunner Scowcroft in the wreckage of one of the shelters on the old position who had been killed during last night's shelling.

'A' subsection had a narrow escape when a shell dropped just outside their shelter, wrecking it and setting fire to all the propellant charges near the gun, but by a miracle no-one was hurt except George Vallender who was badly burnt by an exploding charge. A second miracle occurred when at dinner time a 5.9 shell hit the buffer of No. 6 gun and failed to explode.

This sort of thing perhaps explains the comparatively low casualty rate with which the Battery has so far been fortunate.

After tea, Arthur and I moved out of our dog kennel shelter into a disused gun pit which was part of one of the recently destroyed positions and we felt it might be a little safer there.

August 16
After the day's chores we were joined by another new signaller called Gee (no relation of Sergeant Gee) and we set to and cleared out the rubble and straw from our new quarters. Unfortunately the side facing the Germans was now open but at least we had a roof over us. The mail included two parcels for me and we were able to enjoy a good supper.

August 21
Received the welcome news that I was to go out for three days rest so, hurriedly packing my kit on the only available bicycle, I rode down to the WL. Arthur followed shortly after and we made a beeline for the canal which at this point doesn't harbour quite so much questionable debris as it does at Pelican Bridge.

After tea five of us made a carefree little party into Furnes for supper.

August 22
Six of us obtained passes and walked to the small seaside resort of La Panne about 6 kilometres away. After tea and '*wads*' at a YMCA the party split up, Arthur Shaw and I to get a haircut, the others to go for a swim in the sea. Dinner followed and then we lay on the sandy beach and relaxed.

This was marvellous and it was even more marvellous when we too went into the water which gave us an appetite for tea at a cafe where a small orchestra was making soothing noises and then a visit to a cinema. It was about 8.30 when we came out and after a little shopping, for the shops were still open, we called at the Divisonal Ammunition Column HQ where I found Corporal Child who did me such a good turn in rescuing me from a Trench Mortar draft down at the Base in Harfleur in 1916.

August 24
Sergeant Gee and I tried to get passes to go to Dunkerque for the day but Captain Eddison would only let us go in the afternoon until 9 p.m. Dinner over we borrowed bikes and set off into a strong head wind. We found it very hard work and when, at La Panne, we realised that Dunkerque was still 20 kilometres away we decided to stay where we were and left our bicycles at the DAC HQ office where we borrowed bathing gear.

There was quite a heavy sea but we went in and had a glorious bathe. Then we made our way to a patisserie to indulge our appetite for French pastries where we found that Ray and Percy Swift had arrived on foot with the same idea.

A visit to the cinema brought the

Are you in there Norman?

outing to an end for the other two who had to walk back leaving Ted Gee and myself with enough time for a stroll along the sea front and a visit to the YMCA where a concert was in progress. We had to leave this about 8.30 but with the wind now behind us we cycled back in 20 minutes to reach the WL before our passes expired at 9 o'clock.

August 25
We had just set off to walk up to the Battery position with the right section detachments who had been out for a short rest with us, when we were brought back with the news that the whole Battery personnel were coming out for ten days rest.

Later I cycled up to collect some of my kit and have a swim. We have a better bathing place than the canal by the billet now; it lies half way to the OP in the flooded area where the water is clear and, being shallow, is warmer. A few yards away is a huge shell crater filled with rather muddy water but deep enough to dive into. Arthur persuaded me to dive into this with my arms down by my side.

'*It's quite simple*', he said, '*Just bring your head back as you enter the water.*' With some misgiving I leapt off the edge and sank below the surface not knowing which way up I was. All was black as I opened my eyes so I began to thrash about until presently the colour grew less murky and gradually through the lightening shades of grey-green I emerged into the blessed light of day to find Arthur anxiously watching the agitated water. Not being a very good swimmer I preferred to wallow in the shallows after that.

August 26
As the guns were being left in position a guard was sent up and in the evening I had to take up two wagons with their rations and to bring back the kit of the detachments who had gone down to the WL. All was quiet as we reached the position except for a few shrapnel shells on the road; we loaded up and came away without delay. Then the rain came down in torrents and we were all soaked to the skin. It was pitch dark as we raced along the canal bank and I quite expected a smash up on the cratered road but all was well until just after reaching the WL a wheel came off one wagon.

August 31
I have always detested the routine at WL and here I managed to find jobs which kept me away from '*Stables*' as much as possible. One quite pleasant occupation for a couple of wet days was to paint the drivers' names on little boards to hang

above their harness on the racks.

The telephone lines at the position had to be kept in reasonable repair and it was my turn today with another signaller so we cycled up and took some food with us.

September 2
The WL is to move to a new position amongst the sand dunes near the beach.

Sergeant Gee learned that he had been awarded the Military Medal and we both had instructions to present ourselves at Brigade HQ for an interview with the Colonel in connection with our applications for commissions. We seemed to ride for miles before we located HQ and for more miles before we could find our new WL which was now somewhere in that vast area of dunes.

September 3
I went on early morning exercising order down to the beach. Riding one horse and leading another we rode into the water and as far as the eye could see along the sands were hundreds of others doing the same thing. Both horses and riders enjoyed themselves spashing about in the sea but here and there a timid animal would shy at the white breakers.

After dinner, orders came for the guns to be manned again. The gunners and signallers rode up in a body to within half a mile of the position and then had to proceed on foot as the road from there was under observation from German balloons.

Shortly after our arrival Ray was hit on the head by a shell splinter but his steel helmet saved him from serious injury.

September 4
Booked for lines today with Gunner Gee and in spite of their having been patrolled while we were out on rest the OP line was blown to bits. We made an early start at 5.30 but we were still working on it when Major Petrie who is now back with the Battery, passed on his way to the OP. As he was unable to do any shooting we all returned about mid-day to get some food – for Gee and I this was breakfast – before having another go at the line. It was 7.30 p.m. before we crept back utterly weary and famished to find there was no food left. We had to content ourselves with a hard-tack biscuit and a mug of cold tea from the bottom of a dixie which we shared.

September 5
Felt more hopeful as I set off for my turn at the OP since the linesmen of the day had reported the line OK but I was a little too optimistic and should have known better. Soon after I left the position *Fritz* started to shell 'T' Battery, a regular RHA unit, lying about 200 yards in front of us.

Our telephone line ran quite close to them and sure enough we were unable to get through from the OP and I set off back to look for the break. When I got within sight of 'T' Battery I could see that the whole position was being ruthlessly blown to bits with 5.9s. It was a horrible sight and there was no possibility of repairing the line just then; I made a detour back to the Battery until it quietened down when we put in a new length of wire to enable the FOO (Forward Observation Officer) to fire a few rounds.

While this was going on the camouflage netting over one of 'T' Battery's guns caught fire and a party of our gunners led by Captain Eddison rushed forward to help in dragging out the gun and moving piles of shells which were in danger of blowing up.

During the evening *Fritz* at last succeeded in smashing up Pelican Bridge with 8 inch shells.

September 6, 7
There was a rumour that the Battery is going out of action tomorrow and sure enough about 5 o'clock two officers and some signallers from the 72nd Brigade turned up and I showed them round the lines and down to the OP where they intended staying the night. I snatched a final dip in the flooded area and dumped my kit in a GS wagon which had come up for stores.

At 9 p.m. the OP line went and two of our men went out on it with two of the relieving signallers. the teams came up and pulled out the guns and the position vacated except for Corporal Webster and I who were left behind to wait for the missing men.

Hour after hour passed without a sign of the linesmen and at 4.30 a.m. we set out to look for them, we found them at last fast asleep in a dugout where they had taken refuge from the shelling. Back at the billet we found enough food for a meal in the officers mess and then slept until midday when we walked back to the WL thankful to see the last of the old gasometer in Nieuport which had stared us in the face for the last six weeks. To the old saying 'Any port in a storm' we now added the qualifying 'but not Nieuport'.

September 8
Went with a billeting party to where our next halt was to be. Leaving the dunes we followed the hard sands along the shore as far as Bray Dunes where we struck inland through Ghyveldt to Uxem.

Here billets for the Battery were arranged and after the horses had been fed, 'Trump' and I returned to the WL in the dunes to act as guides. The transport wagons left fairly soon with 'Trump' while I had to wait for darkness to guide the Battery, reaching Uxem at 1.45 a.m. I was scared stiff that I would miss the point where we had to turn inland away from the beach as one dune looked very much like another in the dark.

September 9
It looks as if the whole Division is going to move again as Sergeant Gee and I were sent out on bikes to find a short cut to the rendezvous for tomorrow's trek. It seems I'm becoming a sort of general guide but perhaps it is just the kindly OC's way of giving us a bit of practice since we have both applied for commissions.

September 10–12
The Brigade pulled in for the night near Wormhoudt where we had stopped on our way up to Nieuport, moving on through Steenvoorde to our destination between St. Jans Cappel and Locre.

The county here is quite different being hilly and well wooded and the horse lines of the Brigade are set out on the eastern slope of one of the hills.

The guns moved up into action again on the Messines Ridge near Wytschaete. This is the very first time I have not gone with the Battery into action. True, I was not with the guns at Arras, having met with an accident on the way, but I did set off with them.

September 13
I was given the job of taking a GS wagon to collect some timber from the RE dump about 5 or 6 kilometres in front, in fact it was just behind the old front line before the Ridge was captured and must have been quite close to where the Battery had gone into action.

We passed through Kemmel and everywhere are signs of great preparation for attack; narrow gauge railways are being laid down and train loads of ammunition are being hauled up to the front. Passing down what had been an avenue of trees overlooking the old German front line on the opposite hillside we noticed that the shattered trunk of one had been removed and replaced by a hollow steel imitation tree which had been used as an OP.

September 16
The right section drivers set off on a grazing expedition towards the front, nearly as far as the old front line, and turned the horses loose where the grass had grown up again.

This meant a nicy easy day for us but one of the drivers was taken ill and when the others returned I had to stay behind until the mess cart could be sent for him.

September 17
I was sent with a GS wagon to collect what timber and corrugated iron sheets I could scrounge so I made towards the front where the driver and I dismantled several disused gun pits and managed to get a good load of material for a harness room.

September 18
Sad news from the gun position reported that Jack Randle had been killed. He was 'B' subsection's limber gunner and was killed while asleep in his bivouac by a random 4.2 shell.

September 19
Collected another GS wagon load of building material from old disused dugouts in the forward area.

The bread ration is very small today and a number of men went out in the evening to look for French loaves. Arthur and I had asked several different people to get us a loaf to make sure of having something and of course they were all successful with the result that we had three large round loaves between the two of us.

September 21

Arthur Shaw and I got passes for Bailleul to look for bobbin lace which is made in this district and after we had tried several cottages tucked away in little back streets we managed to buy one or two small items to send home.

A visit to 'The Follies' concert party rounded off the day and on coming out of here we encountered a man called Wilkinson who used to be in the 10th Battery and has now got a good job with 8th Corps wireless section. As we walked back to the WL a number of searchlights were playing about the sky trying to locate some enemy planes which could be heard overhead.

September 23

After the WL was moved to the other side of Dranoutre yesterday I was sent this morning to scrounge another wagon load of timber and corrugated iron sheets from somewhere to make a cookhouse; this seems to have become a regular job for me now.

September 28-29

The guns came out of action last night with the news of one more victim from a stray shell; this time it was Percy Swift, a friend in my subsection who was mortally wounded.

The Battery now moved to a new WL near Watou and I suppose some other unit will have the benefit of all the building material I have been collecting lately but that sort of thing often happens.

Advance parties from the whole Divisional artillery were conveyed in lorries to reconnoitre our respective positions, passing through Poperinghe and Vlamertinghe to Ypres which has been considerably knocked about since we last saw it in 1915.

Beyond Ypres lay the wilderness of The Salient where no buildings remain above ground level and only the shattered stumps of trees relieve the monotony of flattened devastation as far as the eye can see.

We passed through St. Jean, or rather where it had been, to Wieltje which is now just another name on a map where the old German front line trench lay along a slight rise in the ground and here the guns were to be sited just below the crest of the ridge. The dugouts in this trench are to be used to house the gunners and signallers and from here the country sweeps away in front to another slight ridge held by the Germans.

Tonight Gee and I are to go with an officer on liaison duty to infantry battalion HQ.

September 30

After wandering about the featureless landscape we eventually located the people we wanted who were in the process of being relieved so there was nothing we could do except settle down in a nearby dugout and get some sleep.

Breakfast over – one biscuit and a drink of water – the officer took me to look for an OP while Gee went back for some help to lay a line. The whole countryside is one depressing wilderness of shell holes and dead bodies and one can see many derelict tanks with their tracks blown off or stranded in the mud.

Dozens of concrete pillboxes are scattered about together with several larger concrete gunpits, probably built to house field guns which may have been responsible for destroying at least some of the tanks. In spite of having a number of direct hits nearly all remained intact but there was one where the whole mass of reinforced concrete had been lifted bodily from its foundations by a near miss from a 9.2 or 12 inch shell and left to lie at a drunken angle on the edge of the crater.

It was found possible to observe our fire from the Battery position for the first time and the officers mess became the OP.

The OC and the Sergeant-major went forward to look for a likely position for the guns and from their description the job is going to be a tough one as the ground is spongy and one mass of shell holes.

October 4
At 6 a.m. the attack on the ridge in front opened and very soon prisoners began to stream up the road, some carrying our wounded on stretchers. No guard was necessary and they must have been only too glad to get out of it for the ridge presented a terrifying spectacle; it was one mass of bursting shells and as far as the eye could see on both flanks there was nothing but smoke and flame.

The *Boche* counter-attacked persistently throughout the day but each time he was stopped by our accurate gunfire for which the artillery were complimented. Nine SOS calls during the night gave the gunners little rest.

October 6
The fine weather has come to an end and a steady downpour of rain is filling up all the shell holes and turning the whole area into a sea of mud.

Detachments have been working all day trying to make solid platforms for the guns and level a track to reach them from the road. The team horses are bringing up shells in canvas pack saddles as it is impossible to get wagons through the mud.

October 8
Last night two of us were sent down to join the two who had already gone on liaison duty to Banks Farm. It was dark and we had the greatest difficulty in finding the pill box built on the site of a farm which no longer existed in the drab featureless expanse. After a miserable night huddled in a crowded shelter two of us returned to the Battery for some rations.

Knowing the exact position and range of his pill boxes *Fritz*, of course, shelled these at intervals and we were treated to a certain amount of attention during the night which destroyed a signal lamp we had fixed on the roof.

We were relieved about 5.30 and we struggled back to the Battery where Nobby Clark, one of the cooks, had some hot porridge ready for us. We blessed him for this kind thought and turned in hoping for a good night's rest but in this we were sadly disappointed.

October 9

At 3.30 a.m. we were roused out and told to go down to the forward position as another attack was to be made at dawn.

Half asleep we made our way down the Gravenstafel road to where the guns had been left in a line on the roadside which was as far as the gunners had been able to get them.

When the attack opened at 5 a.m. the guns of the whole Brigade had to fire over one another in support of our Divisional infantry.

Breakfast was sent down from the cookhouse a mile behind but by the time it reached us the tea was cold and the bacon fat congealed. At 1.30 we were relieved by two other signallers and after helping them to put up some sort of shelter with ground sheets we went back to the old position at Wieltje.

We felt better after a wash and shave and were just finishing a meal when the signals corporal warned us for telephone duty for the night. This was the extension of the limit and the OC hearing of this, countermanded the order and we got a night's rest after all.

October 10–11

An attempt was made to get the guns away from the road side by all available men with dragropes helping teams of 8 horses but the vehicles sank to the axles in the deepening mud and it all looked hopeless. It was imperative that the guns should be removed from the road, partly to keep it clear for other traffic and partly because heavy shells were falling on some part of it all the time. Next day 16 horses were hooked into each vehicle and with a desperate sustained effort some of the guns were somehow hauled into open positions in the morass.

Apart from one small pillbox away to one flank there was no cover whatever and the gunners had to make what shelter they could.

October 12

The rain was *teeming down* as we set off in the dark down the one and only road leading to this part of the front. Smashed guns, limbers, transport wagons and dead horses and mules were ruthlessly dragged to one side to keep the road clear, consequently an ever-growing pile of destruction sank into the mud on both sides of the track. Shell craters in the road itself were filled in and covered with great baulks of timber.

Running parallel to the road are a number of tracks made of duckboards spanning shell holes or laid in the mud to provide something for the infantry and stretcher bearers to walk on.

Shells are constantly blowing gaps in these through which men can fall in the dark into the flooded craters and the boards themselves become so coated in mud that they are slippery and treacherous. Sometimes one end will sink under a man's foot throwing him off balance and

'Stalemate'

altogether progress becomes more and more hazardous and a constant nightmare.

In conditions such as these our pace was very slow and the attack opened before we reached the OP and even when we got to the ridge it was difficult to locate the particular dugout to which our telephone line ran. In the tumbled ground they all look exactly alike and in any case they are undiscernable until one is quite close to them. We searched a number of these pillboxes before we discovered the one we wanted and since the German counter-barrage was sweeping the ridge we had several narrow escapes from bursting shells.

As day broke the rain was still falling heavily and totally obscured everything that was happening in front; there was nothing we could do but we managed to make some tea while waiting for the weather to clear. At dusk we were called in and we struggled back to the Battery soaked to the skin and dead beat having achieved precisely nothing.

October 13–14
Feeling better for a good night's rest and breakfast we took our blankets and rations for 24 hours and went to relieve the two signallers at the forward guns. Fortunately the day was uneventful and the wires held up during the night but the

rain continues to fall relentlessly and conditions are appalling.

Our relief arrived about 10 o'clock and back at the old position we got permission to go to Poperinghe which is about 10 or 12 kilometres away. By getting lifts in lorries we reached the town by 2.30 and did a bit of shopping. What a pleasure it was to walk on hard pavements and savour the comparative peace although nearly every night these rear areas are being bombed by Gothas.

October 21– 22
Being attached to the Anzac Corps the Battery has been allotted leave passes to Paris for five days for one officer and one man – and I was the fortunate man.

After waiting around at the WL for several days the pass came through and I wasted no time in jumping on a lorry to Poperinghe from where the leave train started at 1.35 in the morning. This took us as far as Calais where I joined up with two Australians and after breakfast at a Church Army hut we went into a park to clean up a bit. Our train left at 12.15 and as it was a civilian train we had to pay our own fares but the comfortably cushioned compartments were an unaccustomed luxury.

Reaching Paris at 8.30 p.m. we booked into a nearby hotel and after a meal I turned in to make the most of a comfortable bed.

October 23
Leaving the hotel I took a room at the Army and Navy Club which had taken over the Hotel Moderne in the Place de la Republique and then I had to report my arrival to the APM near the Gare St. Lazare. I bought a street plan of the city and planned my sight-seeing programme for the next two days.

October 24, 25, 26
The railway fare and the hotel bill had seriously and unexpectedly depleted my slender financial resources and, although I wanted to see as much of Paris as I possibly could, it meant that I would have to do an awful lot of walking and eat very sparingly.

The last autumn leaves were falling off the trees and blowing about the streets; the civilians were nearly all wearing black and apart from uniformed members of the forces only old men and boys were to be seen. An air of sadness seemed to pervade the city and I was glad to make friends with a lone Australian whom I met near La Bastille and we spent the third and last day together. We arranged to meet at the Gare du Nord and travel back to the front together but he didn't turn up and I never saw him again.

October 27
At Calais I found that there was no train up the line until 11 o'clock next morning so I spent most of the rest of my money on a room at the Grand Hotel and the cinema.

October 28
I just missed the first train but caught another which took me as far as Haze-

Forward position at Gravenstafel, Passchendaele

brouck where the RTO said that my Division had moved to Winnezeele and could be reached by a narrow gauge train due to start from another platform. Sprinting round I was just in time to see it disappearing round a bend. So here I was stranded again and spent the night at a Reinforcement billet nearby.

October 29
Caught the morning train to Winnezeele where I could find no sign of any artillery units and at the Area Commandant's office I was told they were at Steenevoorde about 5 kilometres away. Off I trudged again and found Divisional HQ who said the artillery were still in action. My remaining funds were good for a cup of tea and biscuits but I was getting pretty hungry by this time and was relieved to get a lift in a lorry to Poperinghe; the RTO at the station informed me that the Battery was still where I had left it.

I picked up another lift in a lorry to the WL and was grieved to hear that Arthur Driver's brother and Gunner Gee had been killed at the OP during my absence. I felt very bad about this and in some way responsible for their loss.

October 31
As soon as I got back to the Battery I went up to the forward guns with two other signallers for 24 hours. The only concrete shelter here is a small pillbox now flooded to a depth of one foot and very crowded.

Fire is observed from the top of the ridge about 500 yards in front from which I had to semaphore range corrections to the guns with my arms.

November 4
I set off with Sixsmith, one of the new signallers, to visit our old 1915 position at Brielen; the village is completely destroyed but the Herberg de Kroone, our old billet, is still standing and occupied.

Wagon lines now stand in the fields where our guns used to be and of the hut we used as an OP only the corner posts remain; Captain Benn was killed here and we visited nearby Talana Farm Cemetery where he is buried.

November 6
A party of 5 men taking rations to the forward guns were 3 hours overdue and someone sent to look for them found that they had been caught in the shelling and lost two men wounded and some of the rations.

November 7
After a miserable night in that pestilential pillbox we were relieved about 10 a.m. but as the road was being heavily shelled we tried No. 6 duckboard track as far as Spree Farm. Here we were chased by 4.2s and we moved across to a new rail track which is being laid to carry forward a heavy truck-mounted howitzer and we reached the rear position that way.

November 8–9
Some of the concrete pillboxes in the old German front line at Wieltje have become flooded and three of us moved into a surface shelter which backed onto a low bank. It was barely splinter proof but it was more comfortable.

About 3 o'clock this morning a violent explosion woke us all up to find the place full of smoke and various articles of equipment strewn over us. An avalanche of earth had come in through the open doorway half burying the man next to me. A howitzer shell had just cleared the rear sandbag wall of the shelter, cutting a groove in the top edge on its way. A mere two feet shorter in the range and the devastation would have been complete.

After dinner I had to go on 24 hour liaison to join two signallers from 246 Brigade at Korek. This is a very large concrete machine gun post with 180 degrees field of fire on the crest of the ridge in front of the forward guns. Amongst other things it was used as infantry brigade HQ and was a centre of activity which naturally drew a lot of unwelcome attention from enemy shell fire. As the entrances of these pillboxes naturally face towards the Germans, one is uncomfortably conscious that a lucky (or unlucky) shell might come through and burst inside with devastating effect.

From outside one can see across a shallow valley to the next ridge on which lies the village of Passchendaele held by the *Boche* and our job was to watch for SOS rockets from our front line below the ridge and pass on messages to Group HQ behind.

A number of signalling lamps flashing forward also helped to draw enemy fire and altogether Korek was a most unhealthy place and is where poor Driver and Gee were killed.

November 10
Half past four this morning found me on my way once again to Korek with Lieutenant Rushton and Eric Cowling for an attack which started at 6.10 just as we arived. We were supposed to receive lamp messages from the FOO who had gone forward to the front line but he was killed and his signallers returned.

Eric Cowling and I went back to repair the line as it had been broken by *Fritz's* counter-barrage and we had almost reached Korek on our return when we had to drop flat as another storm of shells fell round it killing six men and an officer who must have been on the other side of the pillbox from us.

As I lay there I saw half a torso with one arm attached fall to the ground a little way to my right while all round me a rain of earth and human fragments came down. Amongst these was a book with a hole torn right through the middle of it — a tragic and pitiful detail. It was horrible!

Another FOO went forward to replace the one who had been killed but he too was wounded and his signallers were recalled.

Mr. Rushton sent me back to Wieltje but no sooner had I arrived than *Fritz* started dropping heavy shells on the road behind, one or two falling short and uncomfortably close to the shelter.

November 12–13
Another night at Korek but a quiet one until 4 a.m. when *Fritz* started a heavy bombardment on our front for a short time.

Back for breakfast and a clean-up before setting off with Albert Vallender to Poperinghe but we were not allowed to get far in peace; 3 Gothas and some DFW planes came over and bombed the road. One slight consolation about aerial bombing for those left to enjoy it is that once the load has been dropped one has a respite for a time.

There is usually some sort of transport on which to get a lift and coming back from our jaunt into comparative civilisation we sampled quite a variety. An empty ambulance took us some distance and then we got onto the luggage rack of a staff car until it turned off. Next an empty RFC car followed by another ambulance eased our journey back to Wieltje.

November 18
After several more trips to Korek for night duties over the last few days I was wakened from a well-earned sleep with breakfast by one of our newly joined signallers, a nice little East London greengrocer who had been called up only six or seven months ago. New men seem to come and go and what a change from early days when three or four signallers were considered to be enough to cope.

About mid-day an odd shell dropped amongst a party of men who were loading a wagon with road mending material on the road just behind, killing one horse and wounding another.

About five of the men had slight

wounds and several of us ran over to see what we could do.

November 20–21
From Wieltje to Korek is about 1½ miles and it takes nearly an hour and a half to get there up the hazardous duckboard track.

After another night on liaison duty there I walked back to Vlamertinghe with Albert Vallender for a much needed hot bath and then lorry-hopped to Poperinghe for a meal and a visit to '*The Pedlars*' concert party. We spent the night at the WL where we managed to find room to sleep in one of the '*bivvies*'.

November 22–23
Lieutenant Spencer had just come out of hospital and we took him with us to the Battery; fortunately a lorry conveyed us all the way to Wieltje.

The one and only pillbox on the forward gun position received a direct hit on the roof blowing in lumps of concrete from the ceiling. Charlie Shaw, one of the original drivers who came to France in 1915, was sitting directly underneath and had his neck broken. Several others inside were slightly wounded.

November 27
A railway mounted 12 inch howitzer has been moved forward about half a mile on the newly laid track, its place being taken by a 12 inch gun which is quite close to our rear position, in fact the pillbox housing the officers mess had to be blown up to make room for the new line. We walked over to have a look at it and its 6 or 7 cwt shells look as if they could do some damage.

December 2
After a final hectic night at Korek I got back to the rear position to find that the Battery is being relieved.

Wieltje is getting more and more unhealthy as the activity round the 12 inch gun attracted more attention from high velocity shells and we were not at all sorry to leave the place.

The new battery took over our guns as it was almost impossible to move them and having dumped our equipment and kit on a GS wagon we walked back to the WL where an extraordinary scene was taking place. Everybody was shaking hands with everybody else and laughing and joking as if the war had ended. So great was our relief at leaving behind over two months of the most gruelling action we had so far endured.

December 3
Leaving the WL the Battery turned south at Vlamertinghe through Westoutre to Bailleul where we halted for a short rest. As we stood in the square a lorry carrying the advance party and cooks came along so I jumped aboard. Our destination was a small hamlet called Sec Bois about six kilometres from Hazebrouck.

December 13
The quiet days are now filled with the

usual routine of cleaning, polishing and checking equipment.

All through the day *Fritz* has been sending over us heavy shells into Hazebrouck and many of the inhabitants are evacuating the town. The mess cart was caught while collecting stores and mail in the town and the horse wounded; the driver had to walk back for another horse to collect the cart.

December 16

Rugger and soccer matches are being organised and visits to Vieux Berquin to see the '*Tykes*' and buy Christmas cards and presents to send home, fill the off-duty hours.

The horse lines are in a side road and at 3 a.m. during my tour of guard duty I found the centre section picket rope broken and all the horses loose in the adjoining fields. I discovered the picket asleep in his billet and had to turf him out and tick him off.

December 20

I was offered a bed at the farm where Ray and Arthur Shaw have installed themselves and spent a comfortable evening there.

Our hostess was a dear old soul called Maria who makes us very welcome and provides coffee whenever we want it.

A short distance away is a cottage owned by another dear old soul called Marie where we have an occasional meal and as these two ladies are rather jealous of each other we have to be very careful not to offend them by making more requests of one than of the other.

December 25 – *Christmas Day*

I attended a Communion Service in the village hall where, later in the day, we were to have our Christmas dinner and concert.

This was the usual roast pork and trimmings served by the officers and was particularly appreciated and enjoyed this time.

As we went back to our various billets the snow was falling.

December 26

Snow continued to fall at intervals all day and in the evening five of us old friends sat down to a little private dinner of our own in Marie's cottage. She had cooked us a very nice meal of soup and chicken to which we added various contributions from our parcels.

The officers were also having a special dinner for which I had designed a menu card and after we had finished at Marie's about 9 o'clock I went along and had another meal of turkey and plum pudding in the mess kitchen. Leaving about 11.30 I escorted one of the officers to his billet as his movements seemed to be a little uncertain in the snow.

And so another year of war is coming to an end as I look forward to leave which is due to come through any time now.

1918: *Things look rather black*

January 3–20

My leave warrant came through and I left Caestre to reach Calais at 7 o'clock next morning where all the leave men were marched up to the rest camp in a howling snowstorm. Things looked rather black as the camp was full of men who had been held up for two or three days but the following afternoon our passes were stamped with the date and we were all marched down to the boat; once aboard we felt much happier.

I returned from leave to find the Battery had moved to a village called Le Menegat where I found a billet in the Battery office which occupied a room in an estaminet.

January 25

The Divisional sports started today at nearby Noordpeene in which the main event is a series of five men a side soccer matches playing five minutes each way. Wrestling on horseback between teams of eight men provided a few thrills and casualties together with tug-of-war and various comic races.

January 27

Following a church parade in the morning the sports were completed in the afternoon and the medals and prizes were distributed by the GOC Division.

After playing three matches in quick succession the Battery team were thoroughly exhausted but they won the championship.

January 28

Ray and I obtained permission to walk to Arneke to visit the Declercks where we were billetted in 1916. Only Madam Declerck was at home but about 5.30 the two little girls Marie and Suzanne returned from school and simply smothered us with hugs and kisses. Soon after M. Declerck came in and we spent a very enjoyable evening with this delightful family.

Arthur Shaw returned from leave with a violin he had made from a cigar box; with a very ingenious folding bow, we expect to have some musical entertainment.

January 30

The Battery met a team from 'B' Battery in an '*Alarm Race*'. This entailed taking off the six horses tethered to a line between the gun and limber, harnessing them up to the limber, hooking in the gun and driving between two sets of pegs to a point where the gun is brought into action; one round of blank is fired and the detachment is fallen in behind.

Our team did it in the shortest time of 4 minutes 40 seconds but lost points over harness fitting and knocking down pegs and so lost the prize.

February 3

We had a visit from Alf Richardson, another old school friend now in the RFC stationed at Berguette. He arrived in a car and took three of us for a ride round the countryside. This was more comfortable than sitting on the luggage rack as we did some weeks ago getting a lift from Poperinghe to Wieltje.

On our return we found one of the younger members of our school days boy scout group called Rawlinson had come over from Arneke to see us; he is in the RAMC.

February 22–23
After days of training, sports and general refitting the whole Division moved through Cassel, Bailleul to Westoutre where we pulled in for the night. Being in charge of the guard I did not get much sleep and we resumed our march next morning but only for a short distance to Kruisstraat, between Dickebusch and Ypres, where we established the WL.

The battery commanders went forward to find their allotted gun positions and Major Day of B/245 battery was killed and another officer wounded.

February 24
The right and centre sections went up into action at 5 a.m. and I followed with a GS wagon and the mess cart at about 9.00.

The position is just behind the crest of a low hill between Polygon Wood and Zillebeke Lake called Westhoek Ridge. We took over from a New Zealand battery and the dugout accommodation is a distinct improvement on the situation near Korek.

February 25
After quite a comfortable night in our new home I was sent with three other signallers to a rocket station a few hundred yards in front of the Battery for

24 hours. This was a German pillbox standing above the ground level on a slight rise from which we had to keep a lookout forward for SOS signal rockets from our front line and repeat them by sending up another rocket from a rack outside to obtain artillery support.

We found a deep German dugout in the vicinity and with the aid of some

stretchers which were lying about we made ourselves comfortable and lit a fire. The day and night passed quietly except for an hour's gas shelling on our right but fortunately the wind blew the gas away from us.

March 1

All available signallers seemed to be out on various duties and I went to the rocket post alone. However, three gunners were sent up to me after dinner but all was quiet until dusk when a single SOS rocket went up in front. I dashed out and sent up the appropriate coloured rocket from the rack and within seconds every gun behind was firing away like mad. It was most impressive and I could hardly believe that I was responsible for it. Presently an irate voice on the telephone demanded to know what we thought we were doing since the infantry had reported that all was quiet in our sector.

I still maintain that an SOS rocket did in fact go up and that my action was correct. Anyway whatever harm was done, was inflicted where it was most useful to the war effort.

March 7–8

Went on three days liaison duty with Lieutenant Holmes and two other signallers to Battalion HQ in Polygon Butte which is a large artificial mound honeycombed with tunnels and dugouts and has been a bone of contention between the two armies. Now that we hold it the Germans naturally shell it every day and the approaches are distinctly unhealthy.

We took turns on the telephone all night and in the morning Mr. Holmes took me to an OP in a sap just off a communication trench called Picton Avenue. No sooner had we arrived than shells began to fall in the trench behind us and the rate of fire increased until there was a steady stream of 4.2s and pip-squeaks sweeping Picton Avenue from top to bottom.

The OP had many near misses and after more than an hour of this we made a dash forward into the front line but soon this became just as bad. I pressed myself into a shallow excavation in the parapet on top of some boxes which I discovered contained Mills bombs but there seemed to be no escape from the vicious '*whizz-bang*' of light shells which seemed to barely clear the trench. Some didn't! It looked as if *Jerry* was trying to isolate this section of trench for a raid and I wondered what I was supposed to do, unarmed and sitting on a pile of grenades which I didn't know how to operate. After what seemed a lifetime we risked going down Picton Avenue to Company HQ where we stayed until the shelling eased off a bit.

March 9

We got some more wire from Crucifix Dump a little way behind and laid a new line from the OP as the old one was shot to bits. Picton Avenue was all blown in so we laid the line across the open and after several interruptions from more shelling we managed to complete it as darkness fell. Returning to the Butte for some tea we had a narrow squeak from indirect machine gun fire with which *Fritz* is in the nasty habit of sweeping the entrance at intervals.

March 10
It was a relief to get away from the place and hurry down Crucifix Track and the plank or corduroy road, as we called the heavy timber covering to the original shell-cratered pavé road, to the Battery where a heavy shell had fallen just behind, wounding three infantrymen and one of our gunners.

March 12
Taking sketching materials I set off with an officer and another signaller down miles of duckboard track and communication trenches to the front line. From here we crept down a sap into a large shell crater in no-man's land about 80 yards from the *Boches* and there through a periscope I had to make several sketches of parts of the German front line trench. Fortunately it kept fairly quiet except for trench mortaring which went on behind us for most of the day.

March 14
Having drawn some pay yesterday, Arthur and I walked back down the Menin Road in search of possible dugout canteens of which we had heard rumours and we managed to get a sandbag full of stuff, so we had a good tea and porridge for supper.

March 15–16
Went down to Reutel OP with the Major for a shoot but the shelling was too heavy to keep the line in repair and we had to abandon it and were chased up Helles Track by aerial crumps — those high explosive shells timed to burst about 20 feet above the ground in a cloud of black smoke with a most vicious crack.

All afternoon and evening *Fritz* has been dropping 5.9s just short of Westhoek, the nearest being 10 yards to the left of our dugout and it gets a bit wearing on the nerves.

Next morning we worked on the Reutel line and it held up long enough to register nos. 2 and 3 guns on a pillbox.

March 17
A quiet day at the rocket post until 9 p.m. when *Jerry* shelled all the roads and tracks for two hours while the division on our right were relieving. About 6 a.m. he treated us to another storm of gas shells for an hour and we were glad when daylight came and we were able to take off our respirators.

The latest shell gas makes one sneeze and cough so that one has to remove one's mask; it is then that the mustard gas with which it is mixed takes effect.

March 20
This evening the Battery was firing in support of a raid and 'B' subsection established a record rate in gunfire for howitzers which require two separate actions, one to load and ram home the shell and one to place the propellant

charge in the breech as opposed to 18 pounders where the shell and charge are in one piece. The detachment succeeded in firing 11 rounds per minute for three consecutive minutes.

Soon after that the SOS went up in front and we stood outside to watch the firework display. The shells from the field batteries just behind us seemed to clear our heads by inches. We heard afterwards that the infantry had heard the Germans relieving and had sent up the SOS rockets to obtain a barrage on their trenches which would be full of men moving in.

March 22
In spite of having three RE signallers sent to help repair the OP line the day's shooting was very unsatisfactory. At least the Colonel, who had gone down to watch the shoot, would learn something of the difficulties of maintaining communication from the front line.

March 25
Uneasy rumours of a big German offensive further south but no details. We raided his trenches tonight and captured some prisoners but half an hour later his counter-raid without artillery preparation caught us napping and took some of our men.

March 26
We now have a Lewis gun mounted on a post supposedly for anti-aircraft purposes but in view of the rumours of a German offensive I very much doubt this. However, just before dusk a German plane came over very low and I fired a couple of drums at him which was a new experience for me.

March 27
Some more platforms have been built today in front of the gun pits to give the guns a wider field of fire. This is distinctly ominous especially when Arthur and I went round looking for canteens and found them all hastily packing up.

March 28
Two of us thought we would go down to Birr Cross Roads where hot baths were said to be available but as we approached the place *Jerry* dropped a shell behind us and another just outside the bath-house followed by a few more so we turned off to one side to await events thinking that the baths might be hotter than we would like. Then the shelling lifted onto the Menin Road and hopefully we moved down to the baths only to find that they were closed till the afternoon. We decided to carry on into Ypres and found a canteen where we got a supply of eatables and then succeeded in getting our baths on the way back.

April 1
The Battery changed positions with another battery about a mile and a half on our right — a curious arrangement that, in view of the date and in less desperate circumstances, would be open to suspicion. We had shown their signallers round the lines yesterday and this

morning we walked over to explore the new position.

Arthur helped me to clean out an old surface shelter until *Jerry* started dropping 5.9s just in front and we took refuge in a deep German mine shaft which the other battery had used for sleeping quarters for their signallers. It was a gloomy place needing to be pumped out four times a day to keep it from flooding and we jibbed against occupying this tomb.

The only attractive feature about this position was the presence of several patches of grass – quite a heartening sight in this depressing salient of mud and water.

April 2
Soon after 5 o'clock this morning some 9.2 shells fell round the right section, one penetrating 'B' subsection gun pit and blowing the gun and everything to bits. Poor Reg Russell, sleeping behind the gun, was killed and the rest of the detachment sleeping in a '*bivvy*' outside were considerably shaken but escaped injury. Two new wheels were fitted to what was left of the gun and it was dragged over to a narrow gauge railway to await removal.

April 6, 7, 8
Showed Lieutenant Rushton down to the OP, a pillbox in a front line which consists of a shoulder high parapet built up above the flooded ground and is a favourite target for Jerry's trench mortars. All the time we were there these demoralising things kept dropping round and spattering us with dirt and I was heartily glad when we could leave the place.

Back at the Battery I had an hour's rest before being sent on liaison duty with Lieutenant Sim, a new officer, and two other signallers. As usual Battalion HQ was well hidden and it was dark before we finally and literally ran them to earth in Glencorse Tunnel, an extensive series of underground compartments paved with concrete and lit by electricity.

We slept in bunks which lined one side of the corridors and the HQ signallers looked after the telephone for us during the night.

April 10
Six wagons of ammunition came up, were unloaded and got away without any casualties. All the roads are being shelled and the German offensive is expected to extend up this way.

A reserve position is being prepared and the telephone switchboard is installed down the mine shaft and nearly everybody goes down there to sleep in spite of the flood water and discomfort.

I am detailed with two others to man the Lewis gun and this doesn't sound at all funny to me.

April 11
Contrary to expectations no attack developed this morning in this sector but it is thought that *Jerry* might try to capture Hill 60 which overlooks our position from the right. Sure enough his artillery opened up in the afternoon but

all attacks were repulsed by the 9th Division.

April 14–15
There is a rumour that the Germans had advanced as far as Hazebrouck but had been pushed back to Estaires. I wonder if the old ladies Maria and Marie are safe; their homes at Sec Bois must surely have been overrun if this report is correct.

Our supply of oatmeal has run out and I'm trying to make a sort of porridge with army biscuit and condensed milk.

All but one section have been ordered to pack up in readiness to withdraw. Some wagons came up at dawn to collect some of the ammunition which has been brought up at such risk but they were shelled off with many narrow escapes. The surplus shells have had to be dumped in flooded shell holes and the charges taken from their brass cases and burnt.

The pumps which kept back the water in the flooded mine shaft have been destroyed together with everything of use on the position. It is a heartbreaking job.

At 6 p.m. the guns were fired for 30 minutes and then hauled out of their pits ready for the limbers which came up after dusk.

A new position was taken up just behind Dickebusch and we settled down for the night in a half ruined house.

April 16, 17, 18
As we waited for the situation to be clarified there was nothing much to do and we scrounged some beds from a nearby abandoned camp. Men were collecting all sorts of things from brand new uniforms and boots to eatables and personal kit. I found a cheap gunmetal wristwatch which seemed to be keeping good time and a new suit of pyjamas which is something I had never been able to sleep in, except in hospital, since we came out to France. Somebody brought in some badminton equipment and we played a very unconventional sort of game for a time.

Arthur and I climbed up the half ruined tower of the church in Dickebusch and had a good look round over the surrounding country. Batteries were coming into open action and the *Boche* were putting down a barrage on a ridge in the distance.

Occasional shells kept falling around and one of the gunners, a new arrival, was wounded and died in hospital.

Two spies dressed in British uniforms were arrested near here and we were warned to be on the lookout for others.

Only lack of space prevented everyone in our little room from having a comfortable bed to sleep in.

April 19, 20
Liaison duty again with infantry HQ which was just outside Voormezeele and our observing was done from a mound on which a windmill once stood.

Next morning we moved back about 500 yards to a ruined château to where the centre section had been pushed forward during the night. We found a shelter built behind part of the château wall on the edge of the moat.

April 21, 22
We had to vacate our quarters by the moat as Battalion HQ took over the place; after a lot of argument we finally settled down in another dugout and refused to move again but later six infantry men were crowded in with us.

The expected German attack didn't take place during the night but this morning heavy shells began to fall round the centre section guns and we cleared to one side until it quietened down a bit as no firing was required at the time.

April 23
The limbers arrived about 9 o'clock to take the two guns to rejoin the rest of the Battery behind an abandoned hutment camp.

The signallers took over two of the dugouts on this forward position which we strengthened while waiting for further orders.

April 25
We were wakened about 2.30 a.m. by a terrific bombardment of the trenches and we had to turn out to repair the lines.

Gas shells and HE were being scattered over a wide area and altogether it was a most unpleasant job. I got a dose of gas early on and it was absolute purgatory staggering about amongst the shell holes and ditches trying to follow the line in the darkness gasping for breath and peering through the misted-up goggles of our gas masks which always seem to limit one's vision and movements so severely.

By daylight things quietened down and the gas cleared away but we were all feeling the effects of it and as Arthur seemed to get much worse we took him to the dressing station at Belgian Battery Corner. It was said that *Jerry* had attacked heavily on the right and captured Kemmel but for us the situation remained somewhat obscure.

April 26
Shells had blown holes through the roofs of our dugout and the telephone dugout near the château during the night so it was just as well that we had been out on the line. The morning was misty and a report came in that the Germans had broken through in front. Picking up a rifle and bandolier I joined Gunner Swales and the Major in a move forward to try and get some information about the situation but nobody seemed to know anything and there was an uncanny absence of any rifle or machine gun fire.

It was all most eerie. Eventually we learnt that there were some infantry holding a line in front and we got the order to retire and came into action near Ouderdoum amongst abandoned camps and WLs.

April 27
Went forward with an officer to the old position near the château and prowled around in search of any sign of Germans or any information. We learnt that Voormezeele had been overrun by the enemy and then retaken, so, having obtained a reliable picture of the position in front, we reported by telephone

and returned to the Battery. There was a wide choice of sleeping accommodation here and another signaller shared with me a whole hut complete with beds.

April 29
The crash of 4.2s bursting amongst the huts wakened me and, hearing men rushing about outside, I came to the conclusion that *Fritz* had broken through and was not far away. Jumping out of bed I pulled on my breeches and boots and fled to a concrete shelter nearby which was already crowded to the door.

Salvoes of HE shells were bursting in the camp with demoralising crashes and giving off clouds of gas which made everybody cough and sneeze and three men were wounded.

The Battery was moved to a farm about half a mile back during the evening; after a strenuous day moving stores and working on the lines I found a place to sleep with two others in the farm and slept like a log.

April 30
Went to the OP with the Major but it was a most painful trip as all the skin had been rubbed off my heels when, yesterday morning, I took one of the wounded men to the dressing station in unlaced field boots and no socks.

Got back to the Battery about 2 o'clock and after a bite to eat I had to return to the OP to join an officer and two men who had already set off. Fresh lines had to be laid to a deep dugout which was to be our home for the night.

It hadn't been used for a very long time and was half full of water and foul air but a couple of hours work on it made it tolerably habitable.

May 1
Was glad when daylight came and we moved up to the OP which is one of three concrete dugouts shaped like Nissen huts situated on a forward slope overlooking the village of Voormezeele which is now once again in enemy hands.

The wires gave us a lot of trouble and we were out on them most of the day until we were relieved at 4 p.m. It was a very painful journey back to the Battery with my blistered heels; my clothes were badly torn and a mass of mud owing to a fall down the slippery steps of the deep dugout we had slept in.

May 3, 4, 5
After a quiet day the night passed uneventfully but an uneasy atmosphere of suspense hangs over us; we miss the feeling of comparative security which a strongly held trench system has always given us. Now we feel vulnerable to the massive reinforcement of German divisions to the western front due to the collapse of Russia.

While it was comparatively quiet Vallender and I scrounged a large tub from the farm and heated up some water for a bath in the stable. As it was sheer agony wearing my field boots I borrowed a pair of canvas shoes which made it easier to get about. Two guns were moved forward again and I had the job of guiding 12 wagons of ammunition up to them.

May 6
The people from the farm returned with a couple of large wagons to collect some of their goods and chattels which they had left behind in a hurried departure about a fortnight ago.

They took the bed we had been sleeping in but we hardly felt the loss since we had to go to the OP for 24 hours.

May 8
About 3 a.m. I was wakened by the continuous rumbling of a German barrage in front and of gas shells falling all around the farm. When one burst in the loft just above I thought it was time to move out to a dugout.

Three of us were sent forward to 'C' Battery with a despatch; three were sent because *Fritz* was shelling all the roads and sprinkling all the open country with gas shells and 4.2 *'daisy cutters'*. These were fitted with highly sensitive fuses bursting on impact and scattering shell splinters over a very wide area.

As roads were out of the question we moved forward across country in open order wearing our respirators. About half way there I was struck in the face by a fragment of shell which burst quite 50 yards away. I tore off my gas mask as the hole in it made it useless and it was filling up with blood. Taking shelter behind a wall one of the others put on a shell dressing and left me there while they carried on. As soon as the shelling eased

off I made my way back to the dressing station as most of the gas had dispersed. From here I travelled on a light railway to 101 Field Ambulance near Watou and after being inoculated and given a light meal I was taken by car to the 1st Australian CCS at Blendeque near St. Omer where the shell splinter, which had passed through the back of my nose and lodged just below the right eye, was removed.

Seven days later I left for blighty on the Jean Breydel hospital ship looking rather pathetic with a face almost hidden beneath a huge bandage and wearing carpet slippers, a jelly bag head covering and tunic and trousers about eight sizes too small. For me the war was over.